Praise for
BRING BACK YOUR PEOPLE

"Aaron Scott offers an empathic guide for communicating with the 'Cousin Randys' in our midst: downwardly mobile, largely White friends and family members who, having fallen for the identity politics and false promises of the Christian nationalist movement, are among its many victims. *Bring Back Your People* is sure to spark some of the conversations we need right now."
—**Katherine Stewart**, author of *The Power Worshippers: Inside the Dangerous Rise of Religious Nationalism*

"As the pastor of a Black congregation recently targeted by the violence of White Christian nationalists, I believe *Bring Back Your People* couldn't be more timely. At the same time, this book shares spiritual, survival, and organizing insights for the long haul—and that's critical. Because as we know, America didn't get here overnight, and America won't get out of this overnight."
—**Rev. William H. Lamar IV**, Metropolitan AME Church

"As a progressive Jewish leader who has been impacted by White Christian nationalism and has been organizing against it for over half my life, I want to express appreciation to Aaron Scott for recognizing the need to organize his community and providing a road map for others to join him. *Bring Back Your People: Ten Ways Regular Folks Can Put a Dent in White Christian Nationalism* is an exceptionally entertaining book about a deadly serious topic. It manages to achieve this unlikely balance because of Scott's irreverent authenticity, his sharp analysis, his masterful sense of humor, and his unwavering love for poor and working-class White people. Whether you have a cousin Randy or not, this book provides excellent guidance and concrete tactics to bring the fight *against* White Christian nationalism—and *for* an inclusive, multiracial democracy—into every town, city, and state in the country."

—**Stosh Cotler**, former CEO of Bend the Arc Jewish
Action and anti-authoritarian organizer

"This book manages to be both incredibly funny and, at the same time, concretely useful and urgently relevant. Mandatory reading for anyone needing an anchor, a lifeboat, and a laugh in this stormy political moment."

—**Rahna Epting**, executive director of MoveOn

"You'd think that fighting rising fascism in America wouldn't be funny, but I laughed (and cried) out loud as I read this book. *Bring Back Your People* doesn't give us any shortcuts, nor does it sugarcoat the work ahead of us. It does deliver a legitimate road map—for seasoned organizers as well as for everyday people just looking to do the right thing in this challenging moment. Don't miss this."

—**Erin Heaney**, executive director of Showing
Up for Racial Justice (SURJ)

"An important book for anyone interested in addressing the surge in White Christian nationalism in the US, especially among poor White communities. In this fast-paced, humorous—and deadly serious—book, Scott tells the story of Randy, any of the millions of regular-ass people who wave the flag of God and country. He challenges the White liberal tendency to write off people often called rednecks, and suggests instead that progressives develop a strategy for counter-recruitment, rooted in an understanding of the material conditions of the poor. Scott calls us to examine history and to build genuine relationships with poor communities and address the widespread incarceration, homelessness, and poverty they face. This book is a must-read for anyone interested in counter-recruiting from the White Christian nationalism that shapes this country's history and present."

—**Cedar Monroe**, author of *Trash: A Poor White Journey*

"What can I say about *Bring Back Your People* other than: If you believe we must build a multiracial, intergenerational, inclusive, and peace-loving democracy dedicated to all humans flourishing and a sustainable planet, it is an absolute, total must-read. With anecdotes and lessons equal parts hilarious, soul-crushing, and deeply hopeful, Scott offers analysis, examples, and how-tos to counter-recruit and overcome White Christian nationalism. Be prepared to laugh, cry, and be inspired to organize, organize, organize. I can think of no book more relevant in these dark, dangerous, but also opportune days."

—**Rev. Dr. Liz Theoharis**, author, theologian, pastor, and anti-poverty activist

BRING BACK
YOUR PEOPLE

BRING
BACK
YOUR
PEOPLE

**Ten Ways
Regular Folks
Can Put a
Dent in White
Christian
Nationalism**

Aaron Scott

Broadleaf Books
Minneapolis

BRING BACK YOUR PEOPLE
Ten Ways Regular Folks Can Put a Dent in White Christian Nationalism

29   28   27   26   25   24   1   2   3   4   5   6   7   8   9

Library of Congress Cataloging-in-Publication Data

Names: Scott, Aaron (Pastor), author.
Title: Bring back your people : ten ways regular folks can put a dent in
    white Christian Nationalism / Aaron Scott.
Description: Minneapolis : Broadleaf Books, [2025] | Includes
    bibliographical references.
Identifiers: LCCN 2024008577 | ISBN 9781506494555 (print) | ISBN
    9781506494562 (ebook)
Subjects: LCSH: Christian conservatism--United States--History--21st
    century. | White nationalism--Religious aspects--United States
    Christianity. | Psychology, Religious--United States.
Classification: LCC BR115.C66 S625 2025 | DDC 261.70973--dc23/
    eng/20240511
LC record available at https://lccn.loc.gov/2024008577

Cover photograph © Alisha Lofgren
Cover design by Olga Grlic

Print ISBN: 978-1-5064-9455-5
eBook ISBN: 978-1-5064-9456-2

For my dad

CONTENTS

CONTENTS

INTRODUCTION

This book is going to teach you how to counter-recruit your cousin Randy away from White Christian nationalism and toward something a whole lot better.

Now. I have no actual cousins named Randy. I know you might not either. Do not start haranguing random Randys on the internet about this book, though they may tempt you sorely.

"Who the hell is Randy?" you might be asking. One way or another, I'd wager you already know him. If he's not your cousin, he might be your coworker, your neighbor, your friend from high school. You know who I'm talking about: the one who manages to keep Jesus dangling from his rearview mirror and NRA stickers plastered all over his bumper, with a pickup load of explosive cognitive dissonance in between. Or maybe you're more personally familiar with your cousin Brandy: she shares Moms for Liberty "parental rights" posts online, has been stockpiling essential oils since 2014, and sports a real middle-finger-to-the-law attitude when it comes to germ theory.

Let me say next, in full transparency, that I've had less luck than I'd like to report when it comes to successfully counter-recruiting That One Cousin. You win some, you lose some.

"Then how are you even qualified to write this book?" you're asking. Lean in a little closer and I'll tell you: because nobody else wrote this goddamn book prior to January 6, 2021—and look where that got us.

That day, thousands of Randys and Brandys went wild all over the US Capitol. And January 6 ended up being a mere warm-up act compared to the events that followed over the next few years: a White teenage assassin murdering Black elders in a Buffalo grocery store while they shopped for Sunday dinner; a six-year-old Muslim kid killed by his landlord in Plainfield, Illinois; the Dobbs v. Jackson decision; the three-ring-circus that brought us Mike Wackadoodle Johnson as Speaker of the House. The list gets longer every day.

This is all the predictable culmination of four-hundred-plus years of imperial nation-building on the ideals of racism, patriarchy, and Christian supremacy. But damn it, watching this sick old system fall in on itself in real time while twisted demagogues step into new voids of power is a little too much to take sitting down.

So yes, I still have That One Cousin. But in my extended redneck kinship network of six hundred or so salty crackers, I have made a significant dent. I've talked folks down from the anti-vax ledge, pulled avowed "White pride" folks into multiracial justice organizing campaigns, and once even convinced a hot-headed, ragtag White militia not to shoot me for mobilizing a demonstration to demand police accountability. It's a start, but clearly not enough. You gotta leave your mark too. We all do.

"But I'm not a redneck!" you might be saying. That's okay. Countering White Christian nationalism takes all kinds. You don't need to put on a camo shirt and work boots and pretend to be somebody you're not. The conversation and the work are far more important than a costume.

"But I also don't know any rednecks!" you might say. That's okay too. In fact, the real heavy hitters spreading White Christian nationalism tend to be a lot slicker (and richer) than your average redneck off the street. In fact, the toxic river of authoritarian sludge that is White Christian nationalism has managed to spill its banks and is flooding a school board, church bake sale, county commissioners' meeting, and mobile phone store near you. You've certainly got plenty of people to talk to: other parents on your kids' basketball team, other kids in your high school "ironically" posting Pepe the Frog memes, other people in line at the food bank, your coworker in the "Let's Go Brandon" shirt (okay, he probably is a legit redneck). Anyway, the point is: take your pick!

Maybe you're a staunch atheist or Unitarian Universalist and you feel personally above all these White Christian nationalist shenanigans. But although this crap is exhausting and ludicrous, I'll bet you twenty-five dollars there actually is a Randy or two lurking somewhere in your sphere of influence. But even if there isn't, you still need to go out and connect with one. You still need to flex those counter-recruitment muscles with genuine love and steely discipline.

Why? Because there are a hell of a lot more Randys in America than there are Unitarian Universalists or Sierra Club members—and the Klan, the Proud Boys, or the ReAwaken America tour would be more than willing to give him a ride to their next meeting if he can't afford the price of gas. The time for staying piously out of contact with people you find "problematic" is long gone (if it ever existed in the first place).

"But I'm not White, and this shitshow is White people's fault," you might be thinking. "Also, I'm not looking to get injured or worse by some racist wackjob!" Okay, now that is a legitimate point. If this book has already become too stressful for you on those grounds, give yourself permission to go take a nap or have some ice cream. I'm not here to prescribe taking on personal safety risks you know you can't afford.

The rule in this driver's manual that reigns supreme above all others is Rule Five: Calculate Your Risks. So, if you're saying, "I'm White but I'm not Christian!" or "I'm White but I'm queer/trans!" then this reminder on Rule Five is for you too, accounting for any number of Randy-filled, sticky situations you may find yourself in.

The only bit of nuance I'll put here is that, unfortunately, White Christian nationalist networks—particularly through megachurches, parachurch organizations, the Christian right's funding structures, and a whole gamut of media platforms—have been intentionally targeting communities of color for a long time. And they have made powerful inroads into the mainstream. For one, this is a matter of survival for White evangelical Christian leadership, whose numbers are not-so-slowly dwindling, and who understand that their greatest potential pool of new recruits crosses all lines of race, ethnicity, and citizenship. In fact, the continuation of White Christian power in this country depends on these extremists' ability to reupholster their old and toxic theology into a new, reactionary rainbow coalition that—at least on a certain level—feels welcoming to people of all races, even if it still mostly benefits the White and wealthy.

Ultimately, White Christian nationalism poses an immediate and worsening threat to the lives, liberties, and well-being of the 80-or-so percent of us Americans who aren't straight, White, cisgender Christian men with ample cash to spare. Whether or not you personally decide to start making moves to push back against the spread of White Christian nationalism, it's gonna keep coming for us: for our families, our neighbors, our libraries, our Sunday school classes, our PTAs, our city councils, and more.

So, you can throw up your hands and say, "This is too overwhelming, I don't want any part of it!" if you want. Trust me, I have near-bottomless empathy for that feeling. I feel it daily.

But the fact remains that in the United States of America, at this late hour, there is no "outside" of this situation. You can declare yourself neutral all day long, but you and I, my friend, ain't Switzerland. Your neutrality is worse than meaningless; it is a delusion. Neutrality will only put you and the rest of us in greater danger. At this political stage in the life of America, you've got a target on your back, whether or not you decide to fight back. If you need to work to survive, you're a target. If you have a human body and thus sometimes need health care, you're a target. Hell, if you need to breathe the air on this planet, you're a target. At some point, you're gonna run out of places to hide. It's time to make a more realistic survival plan.

"Who the hell are you, and why am I arguing with you already? The book hasn't even started!" If that's what's on your mind right now, GREAT. Hopefully that means I've agitated you enough to get your attention. And this country needs your attention.

Who am I and why should you listen to me?

Hello, friend. My name is Aaron. I'm thirty-nine years old, and I grew up in a small town of five thousand other (mostly) White people in rural Upstate New York. I'm a second-generation country preacher and a third-generation organizer of the working class. I was seven years old the first time I witnessed a pastor get run out of a White church for supporting life-and-death racial justice work. I was ten the first time I watched a church lady get up and interrupt a sermon because the Lord had apparently put a spontaneous hate speech about gay people on her heart. Around the time I was fifteen and sixteen, my classmates started slapping Confederate flag bumper stickers on their trucks—despite the fact that our hometown was a good two hundred miles north of the Mason-Dixon Line.

Yet none of that honky bullshit saved any of us. None of it protected us from being impacted by poverty, environmental degradation, or the drug economy. More than one of those kids flying the Stars and Bars from their pickups were already dead in their thirties. White Christian nationalism wages war on Black people, on Indigenous people, on Latinx people, on Asian people, on women, on queer and trans people, and on disabled people. White Christian nationalism also cannibalizes poor and working-class White people, who are the people I come from.

I have spent the last fifteen years of my life doing very grass-roots, low-budget, and at times no-budget counter-recruitment work. Those of us doing this work are trying to prevent people, mostly poor and working-class White people, from getting hooked by White supremacist and White Christian nationalist networks and ideologies. I am not an armchair analyst. This is my real life, Randy is my real family, and these are the real trenches I've been digging.

You want a more detailed pedigree? When I say, "I'm from Upstate New York," I mean I have seven consecutive generations of ancestors in the dirt stretching between the North Afton Rural

Cemetery in Chenango County and the Gerald B. Solomon National Veterans' Cemetery in Saratoga. You haven't heard of us because none of us ever made it big. We're just another long line of regular-ass people who have done the work, day in and day out, across generations, of trying to hold the fabric of our families and communities together. Farmers, soldiers, union labor organizers, preachers, nursing home workers, and yours truly: winner of the Mechanicville High School Class Day Dance Sparkly Sash, Class of 2003 (this is essentially two steps down from homecoming royalty). The kind of people upon whose backs history is built.

I have lived my entire life surrounded by Randys. I played Ninja Turtles with Randy, changed Baby Randy's diapers, broke into spooky old houses with Randy, got drunk off Hooch under the bleachers with Randy, stole sandwiches from Subway with Randy, watched Randy set his own damn face ablaze trying to take a flaming shot in my kitchen one time when my folks were away—the whole nine yards.

I didn't write this book because Randy is my enemy. I wrote it because Randy is my family and Randy is my friend. Despite the fuckery, he still takes up space in a dusty corner of my heart. I also wrote this book because I have more than a little survivor's guilt. Yes, I've been through some bullshit in my life, but I've also been extremely lucky compared to a lot of my Randys. I got out of town and got to see the world without having to join the military. I've never had to do time behind bars. I've never had to go to rehab. I'm gonna make it past forty and beyond. A lot of my own Randys won't—a lot of them already didn't.

So anyway, not unlike Randy, I grew up simultaneously hellbent on getting out of my hometown and also not able to imagine a life past the legal drinking age. But I guess the Lord had big plans for me, because somehow I managed to do both, abruptly landing in New York City at the tender age of eighteen with the hayseed still in my hair. I'd won a fancy scholarship to a fancy private college and spent the next four years utterly convinced that the rich kids from Connecticut surrounding me were indeed smarter, more insightful, and better equipped to lead than I was. Who was I to pass comment on the minutiae of culture and politics? I grew up going to keg stand bonfires in cornfields with Randy and going to a school that couldn't hold on to a Spanish teacher because we were such mouthy little redneck assholes. Anyway, it took me a full four years of college to figure out the difference between "smart" and "pretentious"— pretention would've gotten me stuffed in a locker quick back home.

Still, college was important for me. It was the first place where I started to make real friendships across lines of race and religion, especially with other scholarship students. This was the beginning of my class consciousness. Back home, nearly everyone matched me in pastiness, and my definition of "ruling class" probably would have been "anyone who owns a car dealership." In college, I also, for the first time ever, had the chance to study religion instead of just worrying about whether I personally was on God's naughty or nice list—and I wanted to study them all. Except for Christianity, of course, because frankly I'd had enough White Christian nationalism (which is basically what I assumed most of Christianity was).

Well, God sure does work in mysterious ways. Because here I was—young, queer, newly "political," and full of piss and vinegar—and I thought, "Let me be really worldly and go study socialism in Central America."* There, I learned a new thing or two about Christianity—so much so that I decided I needed to learn more. So, I went to seminary. I fell in with a crew of clergy and organizers building a movement to end poverty, systemic racism, ecological devastation, the war economy, and the distorted moral narrative of religious nationalism. I've stayed in that lane ever since. And I've had Randy on my mind every step of the way.

I've worked a bunch of different angles. In addition to my many glamorous stints in dry cleaning, food service, and janitorial work, I've worked at multiple redneck church camps and after-school programs for Muslim kids. I've done Medicaid research and welfare rights organizing and worked as a pastor-in-training at a Spanish-speaking immigrant congregation. I've worked in harm reduction and crisis response and served on the national steering committee for the Poor People's Campaign: A National Call for Moral Revival, a movement committed to abolishing poverty that picks up on the work that Dr. Martin Luther King Jr. began (we'll look more at this in chapter 2).

Most relevant to this book is the fact that for the better part of this last decade, I have worked as an organizer through the Episcopal Church in a rural, poor, predominantly White county on the coast of Washington State. You may know it as the hometown that Kurt Cobain ran away from: Aberdeen, in Grays Harbor County. One hundred years ago, Aberdeen was the timber export capital of the entire world. That industry is mostly all gone now. What replaced it? A state prison and a

---

* Guess who was teaching the class? A NUN. I shit you not. More about that later.

thriving drug economy. All the Randys and Brandys my age and younger have been born into a high degree of economic freefall.

In this setting, with a ton of folks facing poverty, homelessness, incarceration, and addiction, I cofounded a little outpost called Chaplains on the Harbor. You might as well have called it "Randy's Place" or "First Church of Randy." We worked as street chaplains there—not to convert anybody but to simply be present with people as they walked through many different versions of hell and toward their own healing and liberation as best they could. All the while, we tried to shine a light on how the world should be and could be a much fairer place for the underdog.

It was during my time at Chaplains on the Harbor that I was privileged to bear witness to the very best of Randy. I won't sugarcoat that or paint too romantic of a picture—he's still Randy, he still drove me nucking futs most of the time. But being on the ground together every damn day in Randy's World, you get to see all the ways the deck is stacked and all the ways that Randy navigates that stacked deck the best he can.

And often enough? Randy surprised the hell out of me.

I know, for example, one Randy with a Confederate flag tattoo who's had his ass beat by the police more times than I can count. And one day, I watched him, in a meeting, share the story of his most recent experience of police brutality with a multiracial group of strangers. I watched him sit back a bit more deeply inside of himself, tucked away behind a dignified, protective mask just long enough to get his story out without breaking down. Then I watched him take a breath and return to his own body once he finished. An intentional sacrifice and service, to share that part of his pain with this group he did not

10

know but had decided to trust because they were concerned with addressing the same violence he had faced.

Another Randy I know: a big Randy. Always the biggest guy on the team everywhere he goes, this Randy is covered in prison tattoos because he spent a lot of time there. This Randy loves hunting, loves fishing, loves working on cars. He's not a big talker. One day, I was at work with this Randy and several other people when somebody misgendered me once, then twice. I saw Big Randy start to get agitated—his head swiveled a few times, and he started tapping his foot. Finally, on the third offense, he leaned in very close and dropped his voice to a low and deadly octave. "Who," he pointedly stared at the transgressor, "do you think you're talking about?" Nobody present for this incident ever got my pronouns wrong again.

Over these years, I have made mistakes more times than I can count. But I have also made some dents. Big dents. Bigger than the dents in the fender of your cousin Randy's pickup truck. And I want to help you learn how to make those same dents in your family and community.

What do those dents look like? They're often janky and never especially polished. But they can pack a punch. Just like Randy's pickup. The small but critical interventions that have made up my life's work have often begged the question, "Is this thing really gonna work?" right up until it's time to hit the gas. And then, VRRRRRRM! You find out what's really under the hood.

Case in point: a few years ago, I had the chance to travel with ten rednecks from rural Washington to Jackson, Mississippi, to learn from poor and working-class Black organizers on the ground. We were not meeting with elected officials or business bigwigs—just everyday grassroots leaders trying to make their communities more equitable. Some of these leaders had rubbed shoulders with the likes of Martin Luther King Jr. and Medgar Evers and were still driving the same old hoopty from back then.

Anyway, the notion of bringing these two worlds together for a week sounds like a recipe that could've gone off the rails real quick, right? Unsung Black civil rights heroines and heroes from the deep South linking up with a team of White and Indigenous Realtree-wearing, chain-smoking ex-cons in recovery (and our dogs). But I'll tell you, the results were staggering. Our folks and the Mississippians connected deeply, almost immediately, across their lines of difference. Why? First, because we discovered so many concrete commonalities in our lives—in our respective battles with poverty, literacy, homelessness, incarceration, and more. Second, because we managed to walk through the week with the kind of respect, humility, and openness that comes with caring enough to truly honor another person's struggle.

Toward the end of our trip, one of our Washington folks—a trailer park resident herself—asked our Mississippi guide whether their networks had done any organizing with trailer park residents in Jackson. She replied, "You know, we haven't. It's mostly White people who live in those parks, and the racism is really intense. But we do need someone to be doing that work."

Without missing a beat, several folks on team eagerly jumped in. "Send us! Those are our people; we know how organize them!" We joked about launching a Trailer Park Brigade of organizers, to which our guide, in utter seriousness, replied, "No, that's not a joke. That needs to be a nationwide movement!"

This book includes a few more examples of the dents my Randy Fam and I have made over the years. Still, if you come across any parts that make you say, "This is crap!" well, it's entirely possible you're right. I have often been badly wrong in life, so take it all with a grain of salt.

There are also a couple times I've been right, however, such as when I said Donald Trump was gonna beat Hillary Clinton and become president in 2016. It's hard to explain how I knew this, except to say that, based on the folks I grew up with, I'd kind of been expecting it my whole life. Clinton didn't have a chance in hell in Randyland. Trump's brash and messy persona, his nonsense story about being a "self-made" rich man, his intentional use of bigoted imagery, his history of sexual violence—none of these set him apart from the kinds of politicians Randyland is familiar with. The ways politics unfolds in mean little towns all over the country are often shady and undemocratic. For most of us from Randyland, the script and the character weren't new; the stage was just bigger.

So I would say this kind of thing, and for months, every progressive I knew looked at me like I was utterly off my gourd—until the morning of November 9, 2016, that is. Then they all looked at me like Trump's win was my personal fault. But last time I checked, I did not have one single political party in my pocket, nor do I own a major (or even minor) media outlet. To this day, those progressive friends are all still talking about how shocked they were that Trump won. They were still leading whole damn seminars and trainings about their shock nearly a decade later. How is this a forward-thinking strategy?!†

So, I figured, why not run my mouth a bit longer than usual? Why not write a book about what these folks missed back then

---

† I have the impossible task of sending this book to print before the 2024 election. Who knows how this reflection on 2016 will land in that brave new world!

and what they risk missing even now? If we want to defeat White Christian nationalism, it's time to take seriously the fact that the approach of many liberals and progressives is not working. This authoritarian movement thrives on disbelief and depends on the incredulous, head-in-the-sand protestations of its so-called opponents. It's time all of us woke up to the fact that White Christian nationalism has arrived center stage and ain't going anywhere until we stand up and chart a new, more loving, and just direction for this country. And when I say "we," I mean you, me, Randy, and all our cousins.

What is this book and who is it for?

This book is for anyone who thinks White Christian nationalism is bad news, wants to do something about it, and doesn't have time or money to go to a bunch of conferences. To do your part in countering White Christian nationalism, you do not need to go to a special training, or have a special degree, or buy a special book (not even this one: call up your library and tell them to stock it or borrow it from a friend).

Us regular people, juggling a couple jobs and up to our eyeballs in debt, are the first and most important line of defense in this struggle. Why? Because we're everywhere, and there's a lot of us. Even though the Randy choir is loud and obnoxious as hell and growing bigger each day, there are still a lot more of us out here who would rather not live in a theocracy controlled by a few pasty White men and their AK-47-toting wives. We've just got to get into step, get in tune with each other, and drown out all that White Christian nationalist noise with our own song.

The volume of that song and the number of people singing it are ultimately the only thing that will win a future society in which there is dignity, respect, and a decent life for people of all races and ethnicities, all religions, all genders and sexual orientations, and all abilities. Your participation in this choir makes all the difference in the world. And we don't just need you. We need you to bring all your people with you. Even your cousin Randy.

How should you use this book?

Think of this book as a roadmap toward that beautiful vision of the future. It's a roadmap to a destination drawn by someone who's never been there because, well . . . no one's ever been there ("there" being a version of this country where democracy is robust and all people are thriving). Still, I do love a beautiful drive!

Each chapter includes a bit of me jawboning about history, religion, my own experiences as an organizer and educator, and what I've learned about how people change. I tie in some real-life stories to keep the headier stuff grounded and keep us all feeling a little more connected. I'll also introduce you to what people in my neck of the woods call "Freedom Church of the Poor." To all my readers whose blood ran cold when you saw the word "Church," fear not. This ain't a proselytizing con; it's an organizing strategy. Freedom Church of the Poor is one potent counterweight to the influence of White Christian nationalism. It is the place where Randy, if he's so inclined, can still plug into Jesus without the heaping side dish of fascism. To make sure you're still awake, and to give you a chance to flex those counter-recruitment muscles, there's an exercise for you at the end of each chapter, which you can use or adapt in your own community, with your own Randy.

Is there a voter guide in any of these chapters? No.

Will you learn about the technocratic inner workings of local, state, and federal elections or governance from this book? No.

Will this author help you make your peace with the Democratic Party as a viable vehicle for social transformation? Also, no.

"But White Christian nationalism is systemic! How can you leave out all the systemic stuff?" you might ask.

And I'd ask you in return: Did your cousin Randy first get pulled into White Christian nationalism because he's passionately interested in the inner workings of governmental bureaucracy? No. *Somebody talked to him first.* Somebody, somewhere, took him seriously and hooked him with a story about the world and his place in it. That story was no doubt a misleading and manipulative one, but it resonated with Randy, and it gave him a deeper sense of meaning and connection than any wonky policy guide on American democracy.

That said, there is an abundance of voter guides, election infographics, and get-out-the-vote efforts already out there. There are also really great how-to manuals on the nuts and bolts of traditional organizing: how to start a petition, how to phone bank, how to door knock, and so on. By all means, use those as well! This book isn't intended to replace or minimize the important resources that are out there. But as you probably noticed, Randy, for whatever reason, ain't reading them. This book is intended to be the bridge between you and him. This book is not so much a matter of systemic change or cultural change, individual or collective efforts. White Christian nationalism's capture of all the Randys is, itself, systemic and cultural. It's the culmination of thousands of individual and collective efforts.

We're not going to bring Randy back unless we come for him from every angle we can work.

Hope?

A lot of people ask me these days, "This all seems really hard and bad—where do you find hope?" This happens when I'm teaching or speaking about my work, or when I'm with other organizers. But it happens by far most often when I'm with church people (let me be specific here: White church people).

This question about hope always feels like a bit of a zinger coming from them, and it usually leaves me thinking, "Aren't *you* the ones who signed up for the job of pumping hope into a broken and messy world? All I did was come here to give you a realistic snapshot of what's happening out there. The hope part is between you and God!"

But over time, I have come to realize that people who ask me this question about hope are, like Randy, looking for a story that helps them feel less frightened and less full of despair. What they're really asking is: Can you tell me a story that will help me feel less frightened and despairing? Can you tell me a story that helps me feel at least a little bit better in the face of the fascistic forces that are successfully stepping into critical voids of power in our collapsing society?

That's a really different question, and my answer to that question is no. I'm not interested in helping anyone feel like they're off the hook right now. I'm not interested in that kind of fake, sugary hope.

But here is my answer, in a few stories, to the question about real hope, and real sustenance, and where they can be found.

Like I said earlier, the first time I witnessed a White church run a pastor out for doing racial justice work, I was seven years old. Before they ran him out, though, he connected me to the most formative political education experience of my life. This pastor brought a bunch of families from our church to stay with Haude-nosaunee families that had reclaimed part of their ancestral land at the height of the American Indian Movement, without waiting for New York State to give them permission to do so. They are still holding on to that land fifty years later, and I'm still holding on to what I learned there: that centuries of wrong can indeed start to be set right by a small, committed group of the very people who were so sorely wronged across generations.

The first time a tiny, aging church lady held my hand in prayer asking God to "end the sin of homosexuality," I was twelve years old. Many rough years followed that: a drinking problem, a couple solid decades of dissociation, and (worst of all) being lost and untethered from my own deep sense of myself. Now I'm pushing forty, and I'm transgender, I'm a pastor, and I'm a dad.

When I was seventeen years old, a classmate handed me a copy of *The Protocols of the Elders of Zion*, the classic antisemitic conspiracy tract. I knew it was bullshit, but I didn't have any of the language to articulate why. So, I just randomly asked him to go with me to a demonstration against the Iraq war. And here's the thing: he came. He ended up dropping out of high school our senior year, but not before he'd bought me a "Create Peace" bumper sticker that stayed on my mom's car for years.

The economics teacher in my public high school hung a full-size Confederate flag in his classroom for, he said, its "historic value." I asked the principal to make him take it down. The principal said he couldn't, "because of freedom of speech." I under-stand now that the real lesson they were teaching me was that the Civil War never ended in this country. It is, ironically, their backward education that kept me grounded in the reality that we have never lived in a "post-racial" America, and that progress in the direction of human thriving and justice is never simply an inevitable outcome of history. Progress is only ever won through immense human struggle by huge numbers of regular people coming together to demand the promise of life and dignity.

These incidents throughout my youth all taught me that this struggle must be waged anew, from each generation to the next. Hope isn't something out there that's already been completed, just waiting for you to come find it. Hope is something you do, wherever you are, with the people around you.

If you are despairing at this moment because of White Christian nationalism's ascendancy, your best shot at hope is to get to work and do something about it with others.

You are alive right now, and that means there is a role for you to play in the work of making a good life possible for you and those you love, despite White Christian nationalism's incessant and overwhelming machinations. You do not need to be rich or famous to do this. You do not need to be the smartest or best-looking person in the room. You will make many mistakes in your efforts. You will also make all the difference. There is a role for you to play, whether you are a fast-food worker, a stay-at-home parent, unemployed, a manicurist, a college professor, a butcher, a churchgoer, a drug dealer, a construction worker, a bishop, an artist, a child, an elder, or even Randy himself.

These are dangerous times, but the times of greatest danger are also the times of greatest opportunity—when change is flickering all around us, when we can bend reality and the arc of justice through the strength of our stubborn, hard-earned hope.

So, roll up your sleeves and let's get to work!

1

Rule One: Come Get Your Cousin Randy

Before we can discuss what we, as basic-ass Americans, can do about White Christian nationalism, we have to answer three big questions.

1. What is White Christian nationalism?
2. Who is Randy?
3. What is organizing?

Once we have unlocked these three mysteries and cracked the secret code for changing America from the bottom up, we can ascend to chapter 2.

A quick note on language before we do all that. I use the phrase *White Christian nationalism* throughout this book because I think it best captures the clusterfuck of ideas, histories, and networks I'm trying to describe.* You might have heard other phrases thrown around describing a similar package: religious nationalism, racial nationalism, White nationalism, Christian nationalism, stuff like that. Each of these phrases have their own nuances, but they're pointing in roughly the same direction.

Just keep in mind: none of these may be the words you want to use when you're actually talking with Randy himself. You have to find your own special touch there, based on what you know works with your own Randy—but usually, more generic themes work better (like "bigotry" or "unfairness").

Question One: What is White Christian nationalism?

White Christian nationalism is a motherfucker. An *insidious* motherfucker.

You want an actual definition? Okay. White Christian nationalism, at its core, is an ideology that says:

* ✳ **America is a Christian nation.** It was founded on "Christian ideals" and chosen by God as a light to the world—the very land itself not stolen but given to White

---

* Also, I'm gonna use a big capital W every time I say White in this book, because that's the kind of Red-Blooded American Man my personal Randy is. And also because I'm following the National Association of Black Journalists' guide on capitalization: "NABJ Statement on Capitalizing Black and Other Racial Identifiers," June 11, 2020, https://nabjonline.org/blog/nabj-statement-on-capitalizing-black-and-other-racial-identifiers/.

Europeans by God. So, if any bad shit happened here (i.e., slavery, genocide, poverty, mass political repression), it's regrettable, sure. But it must have been necessary for the sake of advancing God's intended destiny for this nation.

✻ **In the eyes of God, only people who historically fall on the right side of power and wealth in this country deserve life, dignity, and the right to be on this land.** If you know anything about US history, you know that this tips the scales heavily against people who are Black, Brown, Indigenous, immigrant, non-Christian, disabled, women, queer, and/or trans, not to mention a bajillion broke-ass White people as well.

✻ **Strict "traditional" rules around family, gender, and sexuality must be enforced.** This means, on the one hand, ensuring that the "right" kind of people keep making babies and growing the population in ways that are advantageous for the already-powerful to maintain their power—and, on the other hand, systematically robbing the majority of the population of our bodily autonomy, our freedom to form consensual relationships, and our freedom to form our own families on our own terms.

✻ **There should be no separation of church and state.** And if there is, this separation should only serve to defend Christians and Christian institutions from any and all state intervention. Why? Because in a White Christian nationalist interpretation of American history, the "founding fathers" were Christians, and their main goal was to protect Christians from Big Government, not the other way around.

✳ **Violence toward and political repression of anybody in the way is justified.** As the demographics of America continue to undergo huge changes (such as White Christians no longer being the majority), and as the global economy keeps churning out crisis after crisis (driving mass migration, climate change, and war), the power-brokers of this country will try to hold on to power by any means necessary. Gerrymandering, vigilantism, lying their asses off, storming the Capitol, lynchings—whatever it takes.

Did you notice there was nothing in there about Jesus? This is important. White Christian nationalists will preach at you about Jesus until they're blue in the face. At the end of the day, though, what they actually worship is their own power and right to rule. If they were actually concerned with Jesus and the good news he preached to the poor, the widow, and the immigrant, they wouldn't be pushing policy violence against poor and dispossessed people and cozying up to billionaires.

Now granted, this is what everyone at the top of America's political food chain does, whether they're a Democrat, Republican, Christian, atheist, White, Black, gay, or straight. But White Christian nationalists screw you over in the name of God and tell you to pray harder if you don't like it. That's their real flex, and it's a powerful one. Why? For one, it's got most of us convinced that their version of Christianity is the only Christianity. You can argue with politicians and talking heads all you want. But arguing with God (or at least who people believe God to be)? Good luck! Folks will ride for God so much harder than they'll ride for a politician—and they'll ride twice as hard for politicians who they believe are ordained by God to usher in God's plans for the world.

White Christian nationalism is, at the same time, more than just an ideology floating around in people's heads or shouted out of their mouths. It's also a highly developed and fatly bankrolled social, political, and religious movement made up of concrete networks, organizations, institutions, churches, funders, elected officials, businesses, media outlets—you name it. Those details are mostly beyond the scope of this book, but well worth your study if you've got any time to spare.

So, what does White Christian nationalism look like on the ground? It's a little different everywhere, but you'll often find the same prototype. In my experience of organizing in the rural Northwest, I've seen White Christian nationalism's influence really take off in communities where the local economy has tanked. In my area, that's because the timber industry packed up and moved to the Global South in the 1980s and 1990s, leaving a lot of poverty and ecological devastation in its wake, along with a gaping black hole of on-the-ground analysis of why (and what to do about it). Seeing that void, White Christian nationalists and other far-right networks were organized and ready to step in and say to struggling (mostly White) people, "We can tell you why you're suffering. It's because of the immigrants, and freeloaders, and junkies, and welfare queens, and criminals, and tree-huggers, and baby-killers, and queers who are ruining this country—and that's who the elites of the Democratic Party answer to."

Maybe that message sounds half-baked to you. But imagine being out of work with a family to feed, in a county that has in fact voted blue for most of its history, with subpar investment in higher education because most folks expected to be able to get a decent-wage logging job straight out of high school. And suddenly, within one generation, the jobs are gone, the drug economy is booming, kids whose parents and grandparents literally built the town are homeless and hustling, and there are no other organizations on the ground offering a counter-analysis for why or how this all happened or offering concrete solutions to people's daily crises.

I've talked with other organizers all over this country, and in many small towns and rural communities, there's a blueprint that's pretty tightly followed. Basically, you have one really big church in town, often some flavor of Evangelical, Baptist, or Pentecostal. It's the church that attracts the most young families because it has the most robust children and youth programming. It also happens to be the church that all the county commissioners, the sheriff, and the good-old boys go to.

These same church leaders dump a truckload of money into local (often Christian) charities, basically to give cover to whatever these folks do in office. That way, when they get up to something devious, unjust, and quite arguably un-Christian, they can turn around and say, "You can't say I'm corrupt or wicked or cruel to poor people; my church gives so much money to charity." In one rural county where I was organizing, two county commissioners wanted to send more than a million dollars of pandemic aid back to the federal government rather than spend it on a homeless shelter. When there was an outcry from local people in a public meeting, one of the commissioners got all weepy and (I'm paraphrasing only slightly) replied, "How dare you call me uncaring and uncompassionate? I am a Christian. I volunteer at the local Christian-run feeding program every month with my church to make meals and feed those poor, sad, hopeless bums."

So, in short and in summary: White Christian nationalism is an ideology, a huge set of concrete networks and institutions, and a force on the ground near you (or somewhere close by). It's gaining ground all over the country, and it's coming for your cousin Randy.

Question Two: Who is Randy?

Randy, in this book, is a stand-in for any regular-ass person in your own life who currently buys into some or all of what White Christian nationalism is selling. I refer to him as your cousin and mine, but maybe in real life he's your neighbor, your coworker, your friend, or you. Maybe you love Randy, maybe you can't stand him, or maybe, like most family, it's a little bit of both.

Randy is not so narrowly defined as belonging to one (or any) political party. He might be Republican, he might be Libertarian, he might be a Blue Dog Democrat, he might be Independent, he might be a nonvoter. He might be an anti-vaxxer, or not. He might be Back the Blue, or not. He might have a MAGA hat, or not. But he backs at least some of the same policies and rhetoric spouted by White Christian nationalists.

In terms of class, Randy falls anywhere on the spectrum from small business owner to tent-city resident—which, yes, is a huge range. The main thing to keep in mind is that Randy doesn't hold a ton of power or property as an individual. He ain't a member of the ruling class, even if he fancies himself to be, and even if he's willing to do their dirty work.

Randy might actually be Brandy or Andy because sadly White Christian nationalism is a many-gendered thing. For the sake of this book, I'm sticking with a Randy, who uses he/him pronouns because, alas, he reminds me of a lot of guys in my life. But that's just me. Your own Randy might be your mom, or even your nonbinary roommate who holds surprising levels of hostility toward homeless people or immigrants. The world is a complicated place, and if you can imagine it, it probably exists.

The Randy I'm writing about here is White, because that's my lane and those are most of the Randys I know. But it's very possible you might hear some resonance between this book's White Randy and Randys in your own life who aren't White. Why? Because White Christian nationalism recruits across racial lines, increasingly so each year (more on this later).

Finally: Randy might be a Christian, or he might not be (weird, I know). Even if Randy himself isn't Christian, he's not presently gonna stand in the way of violent, exclusionary policies and rhetoric that are propped up by superficial Christianese justifications. Indeed, he may espouse strong secular support for those policies on the basis of what he thinks constitutes "tradition" or "family values" or "patriotism." If Randy is a Christian, he can be just about any flavor: Evangelical, Episcopalian, Catholic, Pentecostal, Baptist, you name it. More importantly, he can be Christian-ish. He can be a big fan of the music, a repeater of the most popular slogans, and culturally very at home among people who do the same . . . regardless of whether he's ever read the Bible or darkened the door of a church anytime between Christmas 2009 and your uncle Rick's funeral last year.

Your personal Randy may or may not look or sound or act anything like the Randy I describe in these pages. Your cousin might be more of a Brad (Randy's wealthy and well-connected boss, who cosplays the hardscrabble, working-class life almost as fancifully as Randy imagines himself to be a temporarily embarrassed millionaire). If that's the case, then this might not be your book. I know Brad, but I live on the other side of the tracks from him, so someone else needs to write that one.

However, even if you've got a Brad (or another kind of Randy, Brandy, or Andy) on your hands, it's still your task to get to know what makes them tick. No, you don't have to write a whole book about them, but you do have to care about them enough to get to know them. What do they love, and what do they long for? What are they afraid of, and why? Who do they want to be, and what story are they pursuing to find that self? What community speaks to and with them, and in what ways does that community help them feel known? What is harming them that they don't know about or can't name?

Most importantly, how can you offer them something better?

Question Three: What is organizing?

You might think of lots of different stuff when you hear the word *organizing*: organizing your spice rack, organizing your garage, helping your grandpa organize his online dating life. All very important.

But in this book, when I say organizing, I'm talking about bringing groups of regular-ass people together to change the conditions of our communities and the world around us.

You probably already do this on some level. Organizing is not the kind of thing that requires a bunch of degrees or admission to elite institutions. On the contrary, organizing is a quilt stitched together from the squares of all the basic human shit you do already to stay alive and be part of your community and society. Think of the squares as stuff like raising your kids, checking on your neighbors, keeping up with the news, volunteering, voting, and catching up with local gossip at the store, or on Instagram, or wherever it is you bump into the town crier.

As with any quilt, you can't just leave those individual, disconnected, lovely colorful scraps of fabric in a pile, wishing they'd keep you warm at night. You've got to find a pattern or make one of your own. You've got to lay the pieces out so you can see what you're working with, and you've got to thread your damn needle and start pulling it all together.

In organizing, your quilt pattern is your theory of change. How are you gonna bring it all together? What are you trying to do, and why? What's the method behind the madness?

Your needle is your analysis: your ability to understand why certain things are happening and to accurately assess what might happen when you make certain interventions. If you don't keep your analysis needle-sharp through continual study and reflection, you won't be able to keep pushing through to the next stage of your pattern.

Your thread is your relationships: the conversations and connections that help bind you to other people, communities, and institutions over time. These need to be strong, and the work that goes into this part can sometimes feel very slow and repetitive. But if you give up because you're bored by listening to people say the same damn thing over and over again (or because, ahem, you end up doing all the talking and none of the listening in those conversations), you'll end up with a potholder when you really needed a quilt. Good luck keeping warm through the winter in one of those.

Your fingers and hands are your political will: your resolve to stick your neck out and take the time and effort to do something to make your community and society a better place, even at the risk of getting pricked (and you will get pricked, more times than you'll be able to count).[†] Understand that when I say "political" here, I don't mean partisan, nor am I referring to stuff like candidates and campaigns and elections. Politics exist outside all of that. Have you ever seen a Sunday school mom flex over why her kids deserve to be the stars of the Christmas pageant (for the second year in a row, for God's sake)? Everything is political because there are power dynamics at play everywhere. When you decide to organize, you're making a choice to see and assess those power dynamics, and to navigate those waters for the sake of making change.

So, what does all this look like when I'm not talking in sewing metaphors (least of all because I actually have no idea how to quilt)? Let's try a more direct and concrete example of what I mean.

Got a dicey intersection in your town that needs a crosswalk? Organize! Get your neighbors together, turn out a strong and vocal show of support to a city council meeting, draft a petition, collect signatures, talk to the local paper about how important pedestrian safety is, stuff like that. If the authorities don't respond to your demands, keep the pressure on. Help the sweetest-looking, toughest old lady in your coalition grab a roller brush and a bucket, and then hold her purse while she paints the damn crosswalk herself. Should the city dare lay a finger on her, film it, call the news, set up a bail fund, get her a lawyer, and take the city to the cleaners. In a matter of weeks, she's free, the city is paying her legal fees, and you've got a spanking-new court-mandated crosswalk. Bada bing, bada boom.

---

† Your best bet for a thimble: thick skin, a sense of humor, a solid support system, some kind of spiritual groundedness, and a security plan.

Of course, it's always messier than this in real life. "Organizing," in and of itself, isn't an automatic benefit to a hurt community; nothing reeks of opportunism like "advocates" helicoptering in to build their own resumes instead of the leadership and power of local struggling people. I like to heed civil rights leader Ms. Ruby Sales's advice on this point: instead of assuming you know the solution before listening to anyone, always start with the question, "Where does it hurt?"

At Chaplains on the Harbor, we had to spend two full years just showing up for people over and over and over again—in jail visits, and hospital visits, and encampment visits, and free lunch programs, and one-on-one pastoral meetings at Denny's—before anyone actually trusted us enough to talk about stuff like police brutality or contacting the media in advance of an encampment sweep in order to publicize the actions of the city against its most vulnerable residents. This kind of intentional slow build—where the victory is never about headline-grabbing or quick and easy wins but about building up other leaders—is what civil rights mastermind Ella Baker called "spade work."

The word *organizing* almost never gets thrown around when you learn about US history growing up in school, but it's the undercurrent of basically every single noteworthy event. For example, Rosa Parks: she was not a nice, tired lady who abruptly decided to keep her seat on that Montgomery city bus. She had been working with the NAACP for twelve years prior to that day, primarily investigating cases of Black women who had been raped by white men. Day in and day out, Parks had been sharpening the needle of her analysis: in sessions at the Highlander Center in the mountains of Tennessee, at local meetings with the NAACP, and under the mentorship of Septima Clark. She had been weaving her thread with countless conversations: with her

Sunday school students, with interviewees she spoke with during her investigations, and with leaders like Dr. King. Her political will had been pushing that needle forward, stitch by stitch. Over decades, Parks and thousands of other everyday people alongside her—whose names are far less known but whose contributions remain indispensable—pieced together a quilt that changed the history of our nation.

Sounds good, but it ain't gonna work

"Okay, but," you're likely saying. "Those were different times, different people. I couldn't possibly do what they did. Also, my White Christian nationalist city council member told me that publicly funding crosswalks is a slippery slope to communism."‡

Welcome to the United States! This place is like a big, old, haunted house from the movies, full of creepy passageways that defy logic and distort your sense of reality. Lots of very bad things have happened here.

Step one in making change is that we have to stop looking at this country like it's ever going to play by fair rules. Haunted houses don't work that way. Organizing for fundamental change in America isn't something you win if you come at it like you're

---

‡ Man, one thing I have learned in twenty years of organizing across America is that we have got a real low bar for defining *communism*. Spending public money to repair potholes in poor neighborhoods? Communism. Funding emergency shelter so people don't freeze to death? Communism! You can only hear so much of this for so long without starting to feel like, "Hell, if it's only communists who wanna fix my potholes and shelter my neighbors, what on earth is the rest of our damn government doing?"

playing checkers. Playing chess helps a little more, but keep in mind: your chess match is against vampires and ghosts. In this haunted mansion, we have to accept that some of what we see—some of what we are being shown—is an illusion. We have to push past those intentionally disorienting illusions. Making change in America is about getting in those damp, suffocating, hidden hallways of the haunted house and facing the truth of all that has really happened here—all that continues to happen here—and trying to get as many people out alive as you can before you get eaten by zombies like Elon Musk and Jeff Bezos.

Now, as you probably recall from the movies, the people best equipped to survive the haunted house alive are the people who:

1. understand that all is not as it appears on the surface,
2. understand the real risks of this place, and
3. are ready to RUN.

So if your cousin Randy's got a little paranoia, hypervigilance, and some hustle, even better. Randy knows the haunted house better than most because he and generations of his family have been living the nightmare for as long as he knows. He knows every corner and hidey hole. He knows the escape routes. More often than not, I find that Randy is perfectly positioned to be brought into organizing because he already knows shit's not right, and he's asking questions. Even if he's not getting the right answer, and even if he's picked up some bad analysis because White Christian nationalism keeps pumping it into his groundwater—if someone in his orbit actually shows up with a real solution to his problem, he's likely gonna fall in with that person.

Who's to say that person shouldn't be you?

Exercise: Find out what's most important to Randy

Take a minute to flip through the Rolodex of all your own personal Randys. Pick one of them (ideally the one you think you know the most about) and answer the following questions:

* What are the three most important things in Randy's life?
* What does he hear in the message of White Christian nationalism that hooks him?
* If you asked him, "Randy, are you a White Christian nationalist?" what do you think he would say?
* How would Randy describe himself?
* Have you ever seen Randy change his mind or change his behavior about anything? When? What sparked that?

2

Rule Two: Talk to Randy Like You Actually Give a Damn about Him

What are the dangers of White Christian nationalism going unchecked?

History's answer to that question is littered with bodies: the Trails of Tears, the rise of the Ku Klux Klan, the Shoah. If you picked up this book, your mind is probably already going down those roads a bit—and rightly so. New headlines every morning point that way, from the wave of states banning medical care for trans youth to surging Patriot Front activity.

But here is a version of that question that might seem weird or counterintuitive: What is the danger to Randy of White Christian nationalism going unchecked?

I'm not asking this question because Randy is more important or special or deserving of life and dignity than people who are even worse off and in greater danger than he is. Nope, not that. I'm putting this question out there because White Christian nationalism will win if we cannot answer it.

I can't tell whether it's fear or loathing, but there's definitely a deep-seated something among liberals that makes them recoil when I say, "You need to bring your cousin Randy to this party." I'm not saying you need to make nice with him or pretend to agree with him; quite the opposite. I'm saying that ceding Randy and foregoing engagement with him because he's "problematic" is handing him over, gift wrapped with a sparkly bow, to White Christian nationalism.

Does that mean that you should invite Randy over for a beer and then proceed to yell at him for two hours straight about all the ways he's wrong? No. This is also a doomed strategy. But—short of Randy having been pulled so far into the QAnon swirl that you legitimately fear for your safety around him—there is still ground to be gained in maintaining your relationship through real listening. Progressives often come across like they're afraid they'll give credence to White Christian nationalism merely by being within thirty feet of Randy, let alone listening to him talk about his longings and ideas. Believe me when I say, from very personal experience, that treating someone like a contaminant is not going to endear you or your beliefs to them. Especially if that person is facing real struggles.

Randy isn't a more important part of the struggle for justice than any other demographic. But due to lack of progressive investment and organizing in Randyland, he represents a seriously underdeveloped front of struggle. And that's a problem, because most of America (by square mile) is Randyland.

It's also a problem because Randyland holds vastly disproportionate sway over our electoral system. But the vast majority of Randys in those broad swaths of Randyland are not presently organized. The big red blotches on our electoral maps don't actually represent a high level of engaged, politicized, empowered Randys. Rather, they most often represent areas with deep poverty along with high levels of voter intimidation, voter suppression, and low rates of voter registration and turnout. Red counties and red states are not as "unwinnable" as the Democratic Party has lazily framed them up to be. They are uncontested and unorganized.

And there's a "sleeping giant," as we say in the Poor People's Campaign, within those regions. There's a whole army of Randys, Brandys, and Andys with everything to gain in countering White Christian nationalism.

YOU: Like what?

ME: How about not dying in poverty before they reach retirement age?

Case in point: West Virginia, at 93.5 percent White, is consistently ranked in the top five poorest states and has some of the lowest voter turnout in the nation. What if poor White West Virginians, en masse, saw poor Black West Virginians, and poor West Virginian immigrants, and other dispossessed West Virginians not as enemies but as people with whom they have common cause? What might happen then? This isn't a pie-in-the-sky question, either; it's one that countless West Virginians themselves are pushing forward through their own organization with groups like the West Virginia Poor People's Campaign, West Virginia Can't Wait, Keeper of the Mountains, and more.

A lot of people think poor folks are powerless. A lot of people think poor folks are ignorant. A lot of people think poor folks are poor because they've made morally wrong choices. This is pretty much how people talk about Randy. It's also basically the same narrative America spews about poor people across racial lines, across history. Of course, there's always some fairytale of a "good" or "exceptional" type of poor person, propped up in the media or in our churches, basically as a way to smear the rest of us and say we got what we deserved.

Why is it so essential in this society for the wealthy (and the politicians who serve them) to keep poor people down? Not just materially but also psychologically and socially? Easy: they're scared of us.

Here's the thing about poor people that scares the shit out of White Christian nationalism: there's more of us, and our ranks are growing. What poor people are going through today is coming for the rest of the country tomorrow. In other words, most Americans are gonna have to figure out how to survive like poor Americans have all this time. Our economy has been undergoing—and will only continue to undergo—big economic transformations, from outsourcing, to globalization, to automation. We live in a downwardly mobile economy, and the free fall to the bottom is speeding up daily. It's getting harder and harder to hide that reality.

And this is where our power lies—if we can come together despite all the traps set to turn us against each other.

White Christian nationalism's trap for poor people says, "Pay no attention to the man behind the curtain. See those queers over there? Those transgender people? Those baby killers? Those junkies? Those criminals? Those freeloaders? They're the reason your life is shitty. Any policy and politician not attacking them is attacking you."

There are a lot of ways we, as poor people, fall for this lie. Sometimes we fall for it by voting for politicians who ape a working-class aesthetic and racist dogwhistling while passing policies that further immiserate our communities. Sometimes we fall for it by consuming media that plays into these same biases and further brainwashes us into thinking that anyone at the top has our interests in mind. Sometimes we fall for it by turning on other poor people: our relatives struggling with addiction, our neighbors who are already living on the street while we're still one paycheck away.

And sometimes we fall for it by turning on ourselves, believing the lies constantly told about our immorality and our undeservingness.

But what's more important than anything is that sometimes we don't fall for it. Sometimes, and this happens more often than anyone in power wants you to know, even Randy himself ain't falling for it.

Meanwhile, back home

Writing this book took me down a real warren of internet rabbit holes to catch up on the news from my hometown. Once upon a time, Mechanicville, New York, was a big deal: the double-luxe life of a canal town *and* a railroad town, right on the Hudson River. Then that mostly dried up, but it was still a paper mill town. The two old widows who lived next door when I was growing up would tell me and my sister stories about how it used to be: "There was a movie theater! You could hop on the train and ride to Albany or just about anywhere."

41

By the time we came along, there was no movie theater, the train didn't stop there anymore, the paper mill had shut down, lots of the downtown was boarded up, and there was Klan graffiti on the back roads.

So, when I think about whether me and my multiracial queer family could ever realistically thrive by going back . . . well, I can't say I miss it too bad. I miss certain people for sure. I especially miss my hometown best friend, who has been valiantly championing this book to all the folks who went to high school with us, and who texted me excitedly to tell me about the genuine support and enthusiasm people were showing for it.

"Think about the unquestioned support you got from people who you haven't spoken to in twenty years," she said. "The sense of community isn't lost in a town like ours in the same way it is almost everywhere else. Would those same people keep you safe if you came to live back home? Maybe, maybe not. But as far as being bonded, sometimes trauma bonded, it's a unique characteristic of a small rural community."

She reminded me that a sense of community is critical in building higher levels of hope and resilience and pointed out that, in a messed-up way, this can actually make hometowns like ours "even MORE susceptible to the bullshit of White [Christian] nationalism because of their hopefulness that someone will give a shit." And in too many towns like ours, White Christian nationalists are the only ones out there knocking on doors with something to offer.

Still, some days, out of nowhere, homesickness punches me in the gut. Yes, at eighteen, I caught the first bus I could to hop to New York City and never looked back. But I have never been able to feel at home in any big city. I always end up feeling more at home in other messy, broke small towns (evidently, I have a thing for rusted-out railroad stations, boarded-up buildings, and polluted rivers). And there is not one goddamn thing that's romantic about messy, broke small towns. They are often cruel, violent, suffocating places. I just personally find myself psychologically overwhelmed when surrounded by thousands and millions of strangers. I guess it comes down to the trade-off between being liberated and unknown versus being despised and known. It would be nice if we didn't have to choose.

Anyway! As I've been going back and catching up on the news from home, I have to say, the highs did not make up for the lows. Sure, I'm glad that my home state finally threatened financial penalties to force the removal of our racist mascot (a grotesque caricature of an Indigenous person running with an axe). I'm proud of my classmate who barbered the award-winning Best Mullet in America. I'm amused (although wholly unsurprised) by the cartoonishly bad antics of some local elected officials.

But let me tell you, the lows really sucked. There were a lot of deaths: folks gone too soon from overdoses, wrecks, war. There are way more drugs and guns showing up in the police blotter these days than I ever remember seeing before I left.

I also found out that my childhood United Methodist Church building is now home to a classical Christian academy, part of a burgeoning nationwide network of private Christian schools. Though these schools can vary widely in the degree and direction to which they are politicized, a strong contingent of them are devoted to raising up White Christian nationalism's intellectual core for the next generation. A founding presence within those strains of the movement is neo-Confederate pastor and patriarchal theologian Doug Wilson, a leader in the movement to establish the US as a theocracy. Wilson is famous both for enabling sexual abuse and shielding child abusers in his church, as well as for arguing that "slavery produced in the South a genuine affection between the races that we believe we can say has never existed in any nation before the War or since."

Notably, the old mainline congregation is still holding services there in the building on Sundays. This wasn't a hostile takeover but more of an amenable roommate situation.

Something about the transformation of that space—from a mainline congregation to for-profit White Christian nationalist training ground for kids—made a lot of sense. In fact, it seemed almost inevitable, the more I thought about it. I've had several conversations in the past few years with hometown friends who told me they were shocked at the fascistic political trajectories of so many of our peers. Folks they played football or softball with, who were once much more open to people and to ideas across lines of difference, were now walking in lock-step with Team Trump.

I could never bring myself to share their shock. There's all the structural stuff that paved the way, sure: all the steadily escalating global crises that expose the weakening grip of US imperial power, leading to the unmasking of the political and theological violence upon which that grip depends. But even on the level of average redneck small-town bullshit, violence has always been an undercurrent. This "new" turn toward radicalization was much less a U-turn and much more a slight but decisive swerve to the right.

When I was in seventh grade, I sat next to a kid who scribbled swastikas in his notebook and muttered death threats against our English teacher, who was the only Jewish person pretty much any of us knew. No wonder she opted not to live in town. The thing is, that kid's family never would have been able to afford the tuition at this private "classical" Christian school that now sits directly across the street from our old elementary school.

And the other thing is, he's dead now. None of that vile shit—not the anti-Semitism, not the Southern cross on his pickup, not any of the empty promises that White supremacy made to him—protected him or kept him sober and out of jail and alive and thriving. Most classical Christian academies are mainly for rich White kids (along with a smattering of students of color and scholarship recipients, largely to shield the movement from accusations of racism and classism). The power structure of this movement is nearly all White, wealthy men—and that arrangement of who's in charge is in fundamental alignment with their theology of the supremacy of Western civilization and patriarchal norms.

Put simply: there is no place for White trash in White Christian nationalism. We do not belong; we are simply used.

We get deployed to carry out the dirtiest, most violent work of maintaining borders and boundaries.

But what do we have to show for it? What does Randy have to show for it?

I have come to understand that places like the one where I grew up are the intentional repositories of all the willful, unmasked rhetorical and social violence of the US empire. We are the mostly poor and working-class White backwoods, backwaters, and back alleys: the "hidden" places into which the ruling class pumps its most murderous propaganda.

In places like my hometown, then, the ruling class can keep collective despair and anger on a simmer, a back burner heated by legitimate class rage but entirely misdirected at imaginary enemies instead of those actually responsible for our suffering. Then, in the moments in which it's most crucial for our attention to be drawn away from the common cause we have with all other suffering people across race and nation, the 1 percent turns up the heat and lets loose all our honky bullshit. This effectively sabotages any willingness and ability on our part to align with the rest of our class: poor Black, Brown, and Indigenous people.

This dynamic is what allows all those business owners, county commissioners, and pastors who flew first-class to the January 6 insurrection to ape a blue-collar, poor-White-boy aesthetic. But this ain't a populist, working-class movement. Indeed, the sheer wealth undergirding White Christian nationalist organizations is staggering. Turning Point USA alone currently has a budget of roughly $40 million. These folks might wear Carhartt and overalls to storm the Capitol, but it's not because they've gotta hurry back to work at the tire shop once they finish. Back home, they're the same ones calling the cops on Randy when he's down and out and hustling to survive. But get them in front of the news cameras and they're suddenly so concerned for Randy and his kids that they're willing to overthrow the government!

Here's the thing you need to tell Randy (and again, it works better if you're actually cool with Randy, with a certain level of trust for him and from him): they're lying and they still don't give a shit about him. They'll cut off his Medicaid, evict his entire trailer park, and not bat an eye doing any of it. Because to them, at the end of the day, Randy is a warm body in the army at best and surplus population at worst.

But serving as the luckless bootlicker and hired thug of White Christian nationalism is not the only option for folks in the communities like the one that raised me. (Thank God for that.) Pointing Randy in another direction is the work before us.

Who's really on Randy's team?

"Can't Randy fend for himself?" you may be asking. "He's an obnoxiously loud, politically incorrect White man born and raised in all the strongholds of White Christian nationalism." Surely Randy doesn't need our attention.

And yet, somehow, despite spending his whole life in those strongholds, he hasn't reaped shit for benefits. How come? Dirty Open Secrets of America #409,489: Even poor Whites don't get a slice of the pie here.

It is absolutely a fact that due to systemic racism, Black, Brown, and Indigenous people are disproportionately impacted by poverty in America. When unjust political and economic systems attack regular people, they're real strategic about making that attack uneven across race, across gender, across ability, across sexual orientation, across every line of division they can find. That's what might keep Randy thinking that he's something special. "At least I'm not a gangbanger," he might think (because he hasn't been subject to redlining that pushes him into even poorer, more harshly criminalized urban neighborhoods). Or, "At least I'm a legal citizen and I have a right to be here!" (because he wasn't displaced from his homeland by a US-backed death squad). Or, "At least the cops didn't kill me last time they beat me up," (because the Randyland PD might not give a damn about him, but his White skin still reminds them at the last minute that he's some mother's child).

Still, that all specialness hasn't translated to much. You can tell this because when other groups of people organize and assert their right to the American Dream, they aren't looking for a slice of Randy's single-wide pride and stockpile of ammunition. They're looking to live in a society where their voice and vote matter and are defended, where ample economic opportunity exists, where education is free and high quality, where their labor is attached to good wages and workplace protections, where health care meaningfully exists, and where they don't move through their daily lives fearing the likelihood of massive violence upon themselves and their children.

Randy doesn't actually have any of that.

Randy, most likely, lives in a town like the one I grew up in. It might have been a company town, and even though the company closed up and moved to the Global South in the late 1990s (thanks, NAFTA!), the four or five families who raked in the company profits pretty much still run everything: from the city council, to the sheriff's office, to the biggest church in town, to a smattering of smaller local businesses. Anyone who wants a slice of the pie in terms of local money and power needs to make nice with these four families.

Randy probably wants a slice of that pie, but he's got the wrong last name, an address on the wrong side of town, and a record of being on the wrong side of the law. All this leaves him in the out group. He might score a favor for himself here and there by snitching on the right person or roughing up a rabble-rouser, but those favors are always, always short lived. They don't win him better wages. They don't win him better housing. They don't win him affordable medical care, clean water and air, or healthy food for his community. They don't stop the relentless rising costs of living driven by those who privilege greed over the public good. Maybe—and this is a big maybe—if Randy ingratiates himself enough, those favors might win him a one-time stint on the school board as a token gesture. But they will never win him real, lasting power.

On some level, Randy probably knows this. Maybe he stays in the small-town power hustle anyway because it's nice to be attached to some status once in a while. But it seems pretty impossible to imagine another way of operating or leveraging power, especially since the unions have been all but gone for twenty years or more.

But imagine if Randy had the chance to join a big, big team. A team with players outside his town, outside his county—hell, even outside his state. This team is multiracial, multireligious, and fighting for everything Randy needs and deserves in his daily life. This team is out to abolish poverty and inequality, and they're fighting for absolutely everyone.

What would it take for Randy to join?

Well, for starters: SOMEONE FROM THAT TEAM WOULD HAVE TO FUCKING GO TALK TO RANDY. On the ground! In person! You could try inviting him to your wine and cheese meet-and-greet with the candidate you're convinced will make Randy's life better. But he probably won't make it because he's pulling the night shift at the Seven Eleven. And you could try to build a transformative relationship with him on TikTok or some other social media platform, but that won't work either because his rural broadband is shit and he can't afford a data plan. Are you struggling to figure out how to get Randy's attention? Here's a thought: make it worth his while, and don't go about it in a way that makes him feel like shit for not immediately understanding something that's important to you. See chapter 6 for more logistical ideas on this topic. But for now, consider flipping the onus back on yourself for a minute. Ask not what Randy can do for you but what you can do for Randy.

We've got a lot at stake here. Since you bothered to pick up this book, you can probably rattle off your own laundry list of fears and desperations, so I won't waste time repeating all that's making you anxious these days. To be sure, America is full of people like you and me who know that we are stronger together and that what divides us is less important than our shared destiny. But in this moment, we're up against some powers and principalities that have been working nonstop since the Civil Rights Movement to dismantle the few bare bones we have standing in defense of human rights in this country. What we are seeing ripen, from the Supreme Court to your local school board, is the fruit of several decades' worth of networking, church-planting, legal strategizing, electoral engineering, culture-building, media training, and mass political-religious education.

What we are also seeing, though, is simply America. In fact, the hardest thing for lots of people to face about White Christian nationalism is that truly nothing could be more American. Despite their double-speak, the key architects of White Christian nationalist strategy fully understand that this country was not founded on the principles of democracy, equity, and human dignity; it was founded on stolen land, genocide, slavery, patriarchy, and mass impoverishment. "Make America Great Again" is, at its core, an appeal to return to the barefaced violence that built this country.

Do a lot of White Christian nationalists understand this? Absolutely. But are there also millions of people adjacent to White Christian nationalism who don't fully make these connections? Hell yes. There are incalculable numbers of folks sitting in its pews, rolling through its radio stations, relying on its social services—I'm talking about regular-ass people just trying to make it through each day in this mean, lonely country. And that simple fact requires us to understand that White Christian nationalism is not merely taking over because there are a lot of hateful racists in America—although that is certainly true. White Christian nationalism is taking over because, as a social and political movement, it is better organized and more strategic than most other forces on the playing field right now. And precisely because this is America, the playing field is not level. So, White Christian nationalism has almost every advantage you can imagine.

What (and who) have we got to work with?

How do we level the playing field? What do we have to work with when it comes to trying to counter White Christian nationalism? Where is our potential? Where are we strongest? What's the ace up our sleeve?

For starters, there are more than 140 million poor people in this country, all of whom stand to be even more screwed by White Christian nationalist policies than they already are—in everything from health care to housing. But alas, it goes without saying that rabid White Christian nationalists alone are not responsible for the fact that there are over 140 million poor people in this country to begin with. White Christian nationalism is an ideology that misdirects attention from the unchecked influence of plutocrats in every major political party, in part by fomenting division and competition among poor and working-class people. But there are other ideologies in our groundwater that misdirect us in their own unique and sinister ways (cough, cough, neoliberalism—I'm looking at you!). So, among those 140 million+ people, you're gonna find lots of people who are legitimately pissed off at Democrats, lots who are legitimately pissed off at Republicans, and even more who are sick of the whole damn system. That's a lot of pissed-off people. Imagine what they could all do if they decided to unite?

To truly contend with the scale of what we're up against, we need a mass social movement anchored in the lives, voices, and leadership of the masses of poor and excluded people in this country—across lines of race, religion, region, gender, sexuality, and every imaginable line that has been used throughout history to divide us. And one essential part of reaching across all those lines is to find a way to be heard by the people we need to organize.

We need to speak and preach and teach and sing in a way that resonates with millions of ordinary, hurt people. It doesn't matter if you personally believe yourself to be somehow smarter or morally superior to those people, or that you don't like a lot of those people, or that you don't trust them. You have to face the truth that nothing is possible without them. Nothing in this nation moves without the sustained mass participation and leadership of regular-ass people who cannot afford to attend fancy conferences.

So how will you talk in a way that gets their attention? How will you talk with them in such a way that makes them want to talk to you more?

How to talk so Randy hears you

In the summer of 2022, I had the once-in-a-lifetime chance to testify before a congressional hearing on poverty in the United States as a member of the Poor People's Campaign: A National

Call for Moral Revival. This current campaign is a reigniting of the 1968 Poor People's Campaign, the last political project of Rev. Dr. Martin Luther King Jr.'s life.

The original Poor People's Campaign was for people of all races who were facing poverty issues like hunger, failing schools, unemployment, bad housing conditions, and mistreatment by the police. King spent years doing critical work for the civil rights of Black people, but even as he saw changes being made there, he saw that poor Black people, who made up the majority of the Black community, were being left behind. He put it like this: "What good is the right to sit at a lunch counter if you can't afford the price of a hamburger?"

So he started studying and speaking out more on this question of poverty. He realized that it was such a large problem impacting so many people across the country that he would have to bring a large group of people together to fight it. This is why King called for a Poor People's Campaign. He traveled to cities like Detroit and New York, but also to small towns in rural states like Mississippi and West Virginia, and he got in touch with poor people across lines of race—Black, White, Latinx, Indigenous, and Asian poor people—who were all facing the same fundamental problems and trying to make change.

Fast forward fifty-four years later to 2022. Dr. King was long gone, and poverty was now crushing over 140 million Americans—a new Poor People's Campaign was well underway. I found myself seated at a table with immigrant organizers, Apache organizers, experts on anti-poverty policy, and Dontae Sharpe, a formerly incarcerated Black leader from North Carolina who was locked up twenty-four years for a wrongful conviction. It was both one of the best and worst days of my life. The best: because I got to be part of a directly impacted team of leaders across racial lines, unified in our demands of power. The worst: because it was pretty traumatic to spill our guts on camera and have all those representatives and senators tell us all, "Wow, how sad and noble you are," only to exit stage left with no further follow-up.

Then again, we knew we weren't there for them. We were there for us. We were there for our people: poor and working people, of every race and religion and county and state across America. Including Randy.

I share my testimony from that day here because I think it's one small slice of how our movement to counter White Christian nationalism needs to sound, for Randy and for all of us. You might not get to testify before Congress—then again, I never thought I would, so who knows?—but we can all think about the vocabulary that is most effective in our work. Which words and terms and arguments are effective in our work? Which ones aren't? Let's face it: these days, some words are extremely combustible. When you keep it real, though, and talk in authentic ways, you can speak to Randy and to Congress alike.

My name is Aaron Scott. I'm a single father between jobs right now. I'm transgender. I grew up working poor in rural upstate New York, and for the past eight years, I've been helping to pastor a rural, poor, mostly White community in Grays Harbor County, Washington State. A lot of our people die young. Whether it's overdoses, or being homeless in the winter, or police brutality, or suicide—just about all of it ties back to poverty and lack of access to health care. After the timber industry left, we don't have hardly any jobs here.

The reason I do this work is because I don't want people left on their own trying to battle this system the way my family was.

Nine years ago, I lost the most important man in my life, my grandfather. He was an aging veteran of the United States military, and he fell into a mental health crisis. I remember my grandma fighting with different doctors' offices on the phone, desperately trying to get him in somewhere to be seen. But in the tiny town where they lived, in a region with an already overloaded health care system, on VA insurance, it was easier for my grandpa to get a hold of a gun than it was for him to get the help he needed.

He died by suicide in the garage. My grandma found him.

I am here today to ask: Where was the support from this government, that my grandpa proudly served his whole life, when he needed you?

Where was the support for my grandma, his widow?

You left us on our own. It was my teenage cousin and my disabled aunt who had to take care of Grandma in the night when she would wake up screaming. It was a younger veteran who lived across the street who came and pressure-washed Grandpa's blood off the garage walls so we wouldn't have to. He said it was an honor to help our family.

I am asking you to honor the memory of my grandparents Leland and Ivy Scott and fight for our poor and abandoned youth by making it possible for *everyone* in this country to get the health care we need—including mental health care—regardless of our income, ability, immigration, or carceral status. Hundreds of rural hospitals in particular have been closed, and over 400 more are scheduled to close because they're not profitable—that's a quarter of all the rural hospitals in this country.

And make sure we have good jobs, living wages, and guaranteed incomes. We aren't poor because we're lazy. We're poor because the laws and policies in this country are stacked against us. If this can't be done now, make sure we can vote to get people in there who can and will make this happen.

The Bible says,

"Woe to those who make unjust laws,
    to those who issue oppressive decrees,

to deprive the poor of their rights
    and withhold justice from the oppressed of my people,
making widows their prey
    and robbing the fatherless.

What will you do on the day of reckoning,
    when disaster comes from afar?
To whom will you run for help?"

(Isaiah 10:1–3)

I would advise you to not run to our communities for help during election time if you've failed to remember us with your policies the rest of the time.

When you're trying to go deeper with Randy, you need to weave in elements of your conversation that make it Randy-ready. You know your own Randy best, so I won't assume what's most effective with him. In the example of this testimony, however, there are some core components that make it Randy-ready. These include:

* Highlighting a people or cause close to Randy's heart (veterans, elders);
* A clear moral and spiritual anchor (the Bible);
* Describing a community that shares the same difficult conditions as Randy's own (poverty, unemployment, inadequate health care); and
* Compelling evidence of governmental abandonment, abuses, or failures that severely impact everyday American people.

If you've ever listened to or read stuff from that asshat Tucker Carlson, you'll notice he often employs all four of these elements to deliver his own strident, damning statements. But here's where he and I diverge: in our aim and our frame. That brothertucker aims his blame and ire at the Democratic Party and frames taking down Democrats as the solution because Democrats give money to the undeserving (usually coded racism, ableism, and xenophobia framed in terms of criminality) instead of helping "real" Americans. I aim my blame higher up: at both major political parties, which have abandoned struggling Americans in favor of serving those who are already wealthy and powerful. And I frame the solution as a multiracial, multireligious movement from the bottom. Hence showing up to Congress with that whole team in June 2022.

Too many folks assume that Randy will only buy into the aim and frame of despots like Tucker Carlson. It's not true. What's true is that talented despots like Carlson manage to sell their aim and frame because of how they package it. And if Randy doesn't hear his community and his struggle being spoken about on the news anywhere except by despots, then the blame's not entirely on Randy. It's on the rest of us who sit by and let it happen.

Exercise: Why does Randy piss you off?

Now it's time for a little heartfelt introspection. So, pull out your diaries, everyone, and consider the following question:

Why does the Randy (or Brandy) in your life get under your skin?

Is it because of how he treats you or the people you love?
Is it because you've seen him do bigoted bullshit to other people?

If you answered "yes" to these questions, has anyone ever countered Randy on his words and behavior? What happened? What kind of intervention do you think it would take to turn things around? Note: I'm not suggesting here that you're the right person to make that intervention. But it's worth reflecting on who could make it.

If you answered "no" to those two questions above, then let me ask again.

Why does the Randy (or Brandy) in your life get under your skin?

Is it truly because he's so far down the MAGA hole that he cannot be brought back?
Is it because every time you go out to breakfast together, he picks Cracker Barrel?
Is it because you end up arguing about the same shit every time you're together?

Is it because of his social media posts?

Have you ever tried to listen to him about what he finds compelling in his own arguments and why?

Have you ever broached your political differences with him in a way that didn't start as an attack? How do you think this would go?

Spend the next ten minutes answering, with details.

3

Rule Three: Get Real
about History

What the hell is happening in America right now, and how did we get here?

A lot of super smart people are answering that question these days, and if you're looking for the nitty gritty historical record of the rise of White Christian nationalism over the past fifty or seventy years in particular, you should go read their stuff. I'm not going to go deep down in those details, because other people have already done it far better. The dose of history you will get here is one that's meant to be useful for you as you work on counter-recruiting your cousin Randy.

If you want to go straight to conversation starters on history that you can use with Randy, skip ahead to the end of this chapter. If you want to ride along on a wild crash course through One Salty Cracker's Version of The Greatest Hits (and Lowest

Lows) of US History, buckle up and hold on tight. And allow me to repeat the question.

What the hell is happening in America right now? How did we get here?

The short answer: *America* is happening in America right now. We got here by building a country on land theft, genocide, chattel slavery, mass impoverishment of poor and working people, and patriarchy. We got here by telling ourselves the four-hundred-year lie that God wants things to be this way.

The long answer: I'm not a history teacher, but the one thing I remember all of my history teachers telling me, from sixth grade through seminary, is this—empires rise and empires fall. The bigger they are, the harder they fall. The faster they rise, the faster they fall.

The American empire is no exception. Whether a person wants this empire to collapse or not isn't the point. It's already on its way down. You can measure this from all kinds of angles: endless wars and military campaigns dragging on abroad, the steady escalation of social violence on the home front, out-of-control poverty while the wealthiest continue to make money hand over fist, rapidly worsening eruptions of climate crisis, and a doubling down on racial and religious scapegoating as a means of misdirection from our utterly bankrupt political and intellectual "leadership." No wonder people aren't more up in arms for the cause of saving democracy; they're too busy trying to stay alive right now. Plus, they didn't trust that democracy much to begin with.

All that sounds pretty bad, so a fall must be bringing some kind of reprieve, right? Bad old systems tumbling down has got to mean that better times are just around the corner! Oh, how I wish to God that was a given. The unfortunate reality of societal collapse is that just because one decrepit, corrupt order falls apart doesn't mean something better magically or automatically replaces it. Nor does that process of structural crumbling feel great for the most vulnerable. Imagine you live in a roach-infested, asbestos-filled apartment, and suddenly an earthquake hits. Yes, you needed better housing in the first place. But the roof caving in on top of your head could still definitely break your neck.

When old structures and systems are falling apart, it's the forces that are most organized that can step into the new voids of power left open. And yes indeed, there are many old structures and systems that badly needed to go because they were unjust and destructive. Yes indeed, we would do well to organize ourselves around new structures and ways of being together in society that are equitable and create the conditions for all of us to thrive.

On the other hand (as you probably noticed), White Christian nationalism is far more organized than you and I are. It's already doing quite a kick-ass job of stepping into those voids of power. In fact, White Christian nationalism's architects aren't simply content to wait for cracks to slowly emerge along the walls of our social institutions; they're picking up whatever sledgehammers they can get their hands on to turn those cracks into wide-open doorways so they can comfortably and confidently walk on into the halls of power together. Donald Trump in 2016 was the most blunt and damaging instrument they could find, and they used him precisely for this purpose. And the "blunt instrument" metaphor isn't just mine; it's also theirs. The marketing copy for Lance Wallnau's book *God's*

Chaos Candidate: Donald J. Trump and the American Unraveling promises that readers will discover how Donald Trump is a "wrecking ball to political correctness."

But let's back up a little bit further—say, to the 1600s— for the sake of the big picture. What's happening then? Is it all pilgrims and Mayflowers and the fairytale first Thanksgiving? Or is something real goddamn shady afoot?

We need to go all the way back to this time because it helps us fill in questions that exist inside the bigger question of "How did we get here?" Let's look at two "questions-inside-the-question" about the history of White Christian nationalism.

How did White Christian nationalists gain so much power?

The first question-inside-the-question of "How did we get here?" is this: How are these religious fanatics whose plans and policies are so harmful to most of the population (including many of the people in their own pews) able to amass such an enormous following?

First: these folks are sitting on four hundred years of stacking their money. Because of those centuries of consolidated wealth, they also have centuries of consolidated power, all of which has been strategically applied in the last fifty to seventy years to take shape in long-standing and well-funded institutions, think tanks, leadership development programs, educational institutions, and legal strategy infrastructure. We're not just talking about Trump and his high-turnover pack of jackals, and we're not just talking about Congress and the Senate. White Christian nationalists have got whole organizations devoted to building their historical narrative, like David Barton at WallBuilders. They've got rapidly growing Christian homeschool networks that sell a seamless portrayal of America as a Christian nation to the next generation. There are the long-standing outfits, like Focus on the Family, as well as new(er) kids on the block, like Lance Wallnau, who have helped popularize the "Seven Mountain Mandate."

But beyond a long legacy of money and these worst-possible-example dudes, White Christian nationalism has something even more dangerous at its disposal: its historical adjacence to a huge base of moderate-to-conservative White Christians. While it's easy to look at the profusion of White Christian nationalist wingnuts running the show today and wonder what happened to "average" White Christians across America, history shows that this train actually left the station long ago.

Dr. Anthea Butler, author of *White Evangelical Racism*, spells this out simply and clearly. In describing US evangelicalism in the 1940s and 1950s (the heyday of America's most famous White evangelical, Billy Graham), Butler writes:

> The National Association of Evangelicals was comprised entirely of white denominations. Based on theology, a lot of Black denominations would have fit with the NAE, but they were not invited. Billy Graham was talking about communism as an existential threat to America, at a time when the charge of communism was easily tainted with a racial brush, so that anyone who was Black, and working on integration issues or civil rights—including Martin Luther King, for example—was easily branded as a communist. And there's much more. Essentially . . . modern American evangelicalism has been constructed on racial ideas and assumptions, even though these may not always be explicitly stated.

When you're a movement with those kinds of resources and power—paired with deep historical leverage and an insidious presence in the lives of so many everyday people—well, it's very little skin off your nose to funnel huge sums of money both into your high-level targets (i.e., takeovers of the courts via outfits like the Federalist Society) and into grassroots church and community initiatives. While I won't drag their names through these pages, in my years of organizing with homeless and incarcerated leaders, I've encountered a staggering number of charities with White Christian nationalist leanings. I've watched homeless shelters refuse to take in LGBTQ people—or worse, expose them to brutal violence and do nothing to disrupt it. I've seen feeding programs that require people to listen to hate speech against non-Christians before they can eat.

So your cousin Randy has probably been bumping into folks deeply influenced by White Christian nationalism his entire life, at very regular and ordinary events in his community. They're three generations deep into steadily making these moves, with the precise intent of landing exactly where we've landed. And they're not finished yet. They're just warming up.

Second: these folks are also sitting on four hundred years of running a successful script about who deserves life, liberty, and the pursuit of happiness. That script is firmly anchored in race, class, gender, and religion. And it's not just the words they use; it's the policies they set (later in this chapter, we'll hop into the time machine and look at a firsthand example of this). Their script has been in play for so long and has so permeated every institution and structure of society that it's not even strictly the story of White Christian nationalists anymore. A whole lot of people—including plenty of liberals, progressives, and people on the left—have that same script tucked away up on a shelf in the back of their mind somewhere, left over from eighth grade history class or church suppers or scout meetings.

But despite its toxic contents, that dusty old jar isn't plainly and honestly labeled "White Christian nationalism." It's simply labeled "The American Dream," or "personal responsibility," or something that sounds not spooky at all. It is the story of history that makes White people of means feel good about what they've "earned" and the lifestyle they've "created" for their children. It's a story that says God has blessed the wealthy, but the poor are responsible for their own misery, through lack of work ethic and lack of morality.

What's unique, powerful, and dangerous about the narrative of White Christian nationalism is that, despite many of its fabrications, it takes some of the actual truth of American history and says (in a far more saccharine, insidious way): "The exclusionary, violent policies and practices that got us here were good and necessary for the thriving of Real Americans. If you are a Real American, then we did these things for you. If you're still suffering in the year 2024, it's not because of our policies. It's because of the sabotage of those Other People who are not Real Americans like you."

And you know Randy ain't nothing if not a Real American.

Why is White Christian nationalism so appealing?

The second question-inside-the-question of "How did we get here?" is this: What in God's name do all these ordinary people get out of White Christian nationalism?

Think about our cousin Randy. Maybe he went through it for a while in his twenties. Maybe he was dealing with drugs or alcohol. Maybe he was bouncing around from job to job. Maybe Randy is coming from a chaotic home situation. Maybe he's going in and out of jail, couch-surfing, struggling with his mental health, whatever. Or maybe Randy has managed to keep his own life together, but now his young adult kids are struggling with addiction or incarceration or finding a job that pays a living wage. And Randy is doing double-duty, working his own job and caring for his grandkids because their parents can't.

Anyway, Randy's out there in the world, and sure, maybe he's being an ass, but he is also legitimately struggling, legitimately hurting.

What is the one and only community and institution in America that Randy can show up at, with no questions asked, at no cost, pretty much any time he wants?

It's church.

It's church.

It's church.

There's pretty much no other free, somewhat trusted, open-access community space available to the general public in this country besides the library. And listen, I love the library. Passionately. But odds are the library isn't gonna feed you dinner, provide you with childcare, offer you free counseling, walk with you on your recovery journey, pray for you, do your mom's funeral, and weave you into a community that will materially and socially support you through all the ups and downs of life.

So Randy shows up at church. Maybe he's a younger guy, or maybe he's got grown kids of his own; either way, he clearly has a history he's carrying around with him. Say Randy picks a church because it looks big and cool, and there's some message on the sign out front about how we're all sinners and we all deserve redemption. That probably sounds good to Randy because it's sinner o'clock in his life, and he's feeling like he could really use some redemption.

Is this church advertising itself as The First White Christian Nationalist Church of East Boondock? No! That would be a terrible strategy. So, Randy goes inside, and he's greeted and prayed with and fed and welcomed into Bible studies. Along with the fried chicken and potato salad at the church picnic, he's also being served a heavy dose of education about the world, God's will for it, and (most importantly) God's will for Randy's own life. These church folks tell Randy that he matters a lot not just to them but also to God, and that he's called to serve and give back to this world all that has been given to him.

Now that's a beautiful message, and it can change a person. And so wouldn't it make sense if Randy said to himself, "Well, hell. I was welcomed in and cared for, and of course all people deserve that"? Yes, that would make sense.

However, who welcomed Randy in? Was it the social safety net? No, because there isn't much left of one to catch a lot of people. Was it a progressive nonprofit working to defend democracy? LOL hell no, they don't even come to his town. Was it the pretty old brick Lutheran church on the town square with the "We Believe in Science" sign, or the Episcopal church with the cute little organic garden and the high spiked fence? No. Mainline Protestants, I'm just keeping it real—a lot of the time, Randy is not going to feel comfortable walking through your doors because you've got a lot of folks in there who are stuffy and clutch their pearls when he walks by. It's not to say that you all do this, but the vibe is strong. Also, there's just a lot fewer of you. The mainline decline has a real-world impact on the options Randy's got before him. He's looking at about 36 million mainline Protestants versus 100 million evangelicals,

50 million Baptists, and 10 million more Pentecostals, whose numbers are growing every day.

So Randy was welcomed in by his church, a privately funded Christian institution. And the education Randy is going to receive at this church is that this precise institution is the answer to the world's pain and must be spread far and wide, and anyone getting in the way of that is clearly an enemy of both God and all the other hurting Randys out there. And why wouldn't that resonate with him?

Besides which it's mostly coming from the pastor, someone Randy has really come to trust. And if you think Randy got pipelined into White Christian nationalism real quick and efficient, you should see how fast they snatched up his pastor! The sheer number of conferences, trainings, seminars, retreats, and courses White Christian nationalism makes available and accessible to pastors is enough to drown an entire democracy. You can judge the quality of Randy's pastor's education all you want, but that doesn't erase material reality. The cost of attending a mainline seminary is wildly out of reach in comparison to seminaries learning more firmly toward White Christian nationalism. Also, maybe Randy's hardworking pastor just needs a weekend away somewhere. He can sign up for a 50 percent discount (while supplies last) to AMERICAFEST!, the next Turning Point USA pastor's summit. There, he can listen to Senator Josh Hawley tell him how to "stand boldly for biblical truth and the Kingdom" and how "TOGETHER WE CAN RESTORE AMERICA'S BIBLICAL VALUES."

"Okay, but this seems like a pretty niche example," you might be saying. "Not everybody is in Randy's shoes." That's true of course, and it's also true that there are some verrrrrrrry well-off people in Randy's church.* Why does that matter? Because church is likely the one and only place in Randy's life where he gets to cross class lines. Most of the people Randy knows are just like Randy: one paycheck away from the edge, on the edge, or already falling off the cliff. When it comes to class, America is a deeply divided society.

Here's the other thing, though, and it goes back to history: there has been an enormous population of poor White people in this country for four hundred years. And poor White folks make decisions, just like everyone else does, both based on feeling and fact, intuition, impulse, and logic.

The origins of Randy

Poor White folks in the US go all the way back to the 1600s, when western Europe sought to clear out her overcrowded prisons and poorhouses and dump a whole bunch of traumatized, starving felons and street kids on the shores at Jamestown. It was no easy sell to get so many of my salty cracker ancestors to the point that Randy is at today, happy to rub shoulders with the White Christian nationalist elite of East Boondock. At Jamestown, Randy's great-great-great-great-great-great-great-great grandpa, Randall E. Cracker, was far more likely to run away from work and into the Great Dismal Swamp, defecting from the colonial project and throwing himself at the mercy of Indigenous nations rather than starve to death for Ye Olde Jamestown Company Store.

---

* Honestly, that's probably part of what Randy likes about it: rubbing shoulders with the higher-ups makes him feel good, and they don't act like they're too good to pray with him.

And if the leadership of those Indigenous nations told Randall E. that he might have to help them raid the settlement—well hell, why wouldn't he? Randall E. Cracker certainly was not about to give his life for the elite White colonial ruling class that treated him worse than a dog, no sir.

So, what was the trick that White Christian nationalism played? How did Randall E. Cracker turn into Randy? It's a bit like a wolf domesticating into a wiener dog over the slow march of history. It's a con some people call "the racial bribe," and it has been setting poor Randy up to get scammed, stuck, and starved ever since 1676.

What happened then? Bacon's Rebellion was a frontier uprising against the White ruling class of colonial Virginia, where poor White indentured servants like Randall E. joined forces with both enslaved and free Black people to free themselves from labor bondage and get some land of their own. Somewhere between three hundred and five hundred of them marched on the capital at Jamestown and burned it to the ground before they were stopped.

Naturally, this scared the shit out of the Virginia aristocracy. So, what did they do? Less than thirty years later, they rolled out the Virginia Slave Codes. Under the Virginia Slave Codes of 1705, Black people:

* were no longer permitted to carry arms without written permission;
* able to be apprehended if someone suspects they're a runaway;
* had to go through a separate court system for trials;
* could never hire a White person to work for them;
* and so on.

Now, did the Virginia Slave Codes do a goddamn thing to help Randall E. Cracker live a longer, more prosperous life? Not a bit! But they were effective in separating him from the enslaved Black folks he had begun to affiliate himself with. They made him feel a little better about his position because they made life even more hellish for enslaved Black people.

So meanwhile, also under the Virginia Slave Codes of 1705, Randall E. Cracker could:

* continue to live a short, sickly, underfed life;
* continue to not have the right to vote (unless through some act of God he marries into a rich family and inherits someone else's land—highly historically unlikely);
* carry a gun without needing anyone's permission;
* never have to work for a Black person;
* help rich White people apprehend suspected runaways.

Hell of a deal with the devil you got there, Randall!

Anyway, ever since that time, Randall E. Cracker's bajillion offspring have been sold the same script by the White Christian nationalists of the ruling class: "Unite with us. See your future self in our wealth and prosperity. Carry out our dirty work for us. We won't share a dime of it with you, but we'll pass policies that make you feel like more of a citizen than Black people and Indigenous people. And you can even come to our church supper!"

Time-traveling blues

Let's take a look at the following excerpt from Nancy Isenberg's *White Trash: The 400 Year Untold History of Class in America.*

This piece shares words and phrases from the political and religious founders of both the Massachusetts Bay Colony and the Jamestown Colony. As you read, listen for connections between their words and the words and policies of White Christian nationalists today.

The "halfway covenant" of 1662 established a system of religious pedigree. As Cotton Mather's long-lived father, Reverend Increase Mather, put it: God "cast the line of Election so that it *passed through the loins of godly Parents.*" Excommunication alone ended this privilege, saving the flock from a corrupt lineage. Minister Thomas Shepard agreed, projecting that a child of the Elect would be pruned, nurtured, and watered so as to grow in grace. By this method, *religious station enforced class station.* And by celebrating lineage, the visible saints became a recognizable breed.

Colonizing schemes all drew on the language of breeding. *Fertility had to be monitored, literally and figuratively, under the watchful supervision of household and town fathers.* This was the case in disciplining unruly children, corralling servants, and dispensing religious membership privileges to the next generation (i.e. the offspring of the godly). Good breeding practices tamed otherwise unmanageable waste, whether it was wasteland or waste people [. . .]

What separated rich from poor was that the landless had nothing to pass on. They had no heirs. This was particularly true in Jamestown, where the orphans of dead servants were sold off like the possessions of a foreclosed estate. As "beggarly spawn," the poor were detached from the land. Only proper stewards of the fertile ground deserved rights. [emphases mine]

I don't know about you, but when I read this slice of history, I can't ignore the way it echoes loud and clear in the policies, rhetoric, and practices of White Christian nationalism today—in this case, specifically around reproductive health care.

Once we're able to study the White Christian nationalist through the lens of history, the devil truly shows his ass. History makes clear that, for the architects of this movement, battles like restricting abortion access were never about "the sanctity of life" or "what the Bible says" (spoiler alert: the word *abortion* ain't in the Bible). They are actually just the desperate and deadly propping up of a four-hundred-year legacy of White supremacist patriarchal nation-building. In too many ways to count, White Christian nationalism is the unmasking of "benevolent" liberal imperialism and a reversion to the barefaced violence, including mass sexual violence, upon which this country was built and sustained.

Too bad for them, though. Because there was constant resistance then, and there will be now. That's where you and Randy come in.

Could Cousin Randy be the next John Brown?

History is a real destroyer of illusions. It's heavy to study White Christian nationalism and see just how long this beast has had the upper hand. That heaviness can make you question whether any of our efforts to make change really matter in the end.

Funnily enough, though, the secret antidote to that heaviness is actually more history. You know the saying, "History is written by the victors?" That's why White Christian nationalists in places like Texas, Arizona, and beyond are obsessed with controlling the production of school textbooks and every single detail of educators' curriculum. Because the full history of America also happens to be packed with constant examples of regular people fighting back powerfully against a White Christian nationalist agenda.

Take, for example, my personal favorite White Christian American man: John Brown.

YOU: Isn't John Brown the wackadoodle who tried to take over an arsenal to start the Civil War two years too early?

ME: Yes.

John Brown was a lot of things, but most notably a Bible thumper and an enduring abolitionist icon. He was the first person in the United States to be tried and sentenced to death for treason, for attempting to ignite a massive insurrection against slavery. He was also a farm kid who grew up in the boondocks and came from a long line of veterans. He was father of no less than twenty kids—half of whom died before he did, along with his first wife. He was a college dropout and a repeated financial failure, and he was no stranger to bankruptcy, eviction, and debt up to his eyeballs.

This guy—probably half out of his mind with grief and loss and often surviving just month to month—had an impact on the history of this country that we are still feeling today. And not just for the brief parts of his life where he rolled into town with guns blazing. It was also in the way John Brown lived day to day, while he still had to hold down a job and take care of his family.

When John Brown lived in Pennsylvania, he tanned animal hides by day. By night, he helped move around 2,500 people on the Underground Railroad through his barn basement. When Brown lived in Ohio, he and three of his kids got permanently kicked out of their church for breaking the rules about segregated pews. From places like his family farm in North Elba, New York—which I can assure you, as a proud upstate New Yorker myself, is 100 percent certifiable boondock country—he read up on news from around the world, especially about rebellions against slavery in Haiti and Jamaica. And he was constantly sharing about it with the other everyday people around him. In the sticks of Kansas, Brown and his family led several vigilante actions against pro-slavery forces to ensure Kansas would enter the Union as a free state. This legacy made such an impression on Kansas that Brown's image is found all over the state today (and still contested—the John Brown statue erected by locals in the historic poor Black neighborhood of Quindaro, Kansas City, has been repeatedly hit with racist vandalism in recent years).

At the end, when John Brown carried out his doomed plan to raid the federal arsenal at Harpers Ferry, West Virginia, in the hopes of sparking an uprising against plantation owners across the South, he once again failed miserably and tragically.

But even in his failure, which was so consistent with the failures and griefs he'd known all his life, John Brown rocked this country to its core. As a regular, broke-ass, redneck Christian, he lit the fuse that sparked the Civil War. Why? Because all across the country, his actions got other regular people to understand they would have to finally choose a side: against slavery or for it.

What does all this have to do with fighting White Christian nationalism today? I share the history of John Brown because, not unlike your cousin Randy, John Brown was a broke White country boy who loved Jesus, his family, the Constitution, and guns. But perhaps unlike your cousin Randy, John Brown threw the entirety of that constellation—his identity, his values, his networks, his resources, his faith, his smarts, his heart, his actions—behind a sacred cause: in his case, abolishing chattel slavery.

John Brown is important not only because of what he did but also because of the kind of person he was when he did it. He was not a city-slicking, liberal, agnostic "coastal elite" with a trust fund. He was a hardworking, churchgoing, Bible-believing family man, one who would pop all the way off when he saw his values under attack.

So here's the question before us: What if you could get Randy reading the Bible less like his White Christian nationalist pastor reads the Bible and more like how John Brown read it?

What if people stopped telling Randy that he was wrong to be an angry White Christian man and instead said, "You know what, Randy? You've got a lot to be angry about. The way you love Jesus isn't the problem. Your anger isn't the problem. Your target is the problem. You're not aiming high enough. You're not aiming at the people who are causing your problems; you're just shitting all over other struggling people. Maybe together, you and I can figure out how to aim a whole lot higher."

John Brown and your cousin Randy have a lot in common. If you can bring him into a movement that stands for the dignity and defense of all people, Randy may very well be the twenty-first-century John Brown we need right now (perhaps with a little less of the guns a-blazing showdown stuff).

Or if Randy isn't, you might be.

We're thoroughly programmed to view history as something we, ordinary people, can't shape. We're too busy surviving, we're too broke, we're not smart enough, blah, blah, blah. The forces of evil and injustice that we're up against are too big. We need a superhero with a lot of money to come save us.

But history doesn't work this way. Nobody helicopters in to save you, or your family, or your county, or your country. Only ordinary people—in our ordinary lives and ordinary towns and ordinary, boring, shitty little jobs—can save ourselves, by standing up together in large numbers on the side of fairness, truth, and mercy.

Exercise: Spend quality time with Randy

Does your cousin Randy like to watch movies or TV shows? Does your cousin Randy like *you* enough to watch a movie or a show with you?

If you and Randy aren't currently on speaking terms, you gotta figure that out on your own (the exercise at the end of the previous chapter might help). But if Randy's open to it, plan a movie night together. You can each bring one selection. Maybe he'll bring something fun, maybe he'll bring something bananas, who knows. Try to engage and watch his contribution with a critical eye. Ask questions. Then for your selection, try some history. I'd suggest one of these:

* The 2019 historical drama *Harriet*, starring Cynthia Erivo
* The 2020 historic drama miniseries *The Good Lord Bird*, starring Ethan Hawke, based on James McBride's award-winning novel

Harriet traces the life and work of Harriet Tubman as the lead "running abolitionist" of the Civil War era (of interest to Randy: it specifically mentions her direct line to God's ear and her willingness to pack a pistol). *The Good Lord Bird* traces a semi-fictional account of John Brown's life (also lots of talking to God and packing pistols). Both films do an excellent, moving job of showing how people at the bottom of society can lead powerful movements for change. Make sure to give Randy (and yourself) a heads-up that there are quite a few shootouts in both these options!

After you watch together, talk about it and ask each other questions. If you need some prompts beyond "What'd you think?" try these:

* Was there anything you didn't know about history, or just had never thought about before, that this film/show brought up?
* Both of these flicks weave a fair amount of religion into their stories, which is true to the times they portray. What do you take from this movie/show about the faith of Harriet Tubman or John Brown?
* Do either of these dramas remind you of anything happening more recently in America?

On movie night, you and Randy might disagree entirely. On everything. So, expect that. Don't go into it thinking that this is going to be a life-changer, for either you or for Randy.

Counter-recruitment isn't a one-time event. It takes time, trust-building, and relationship-building. You might do this movie night once and decide, "Never again!!" and you're allowed to do that. Maybe Randy isn't ready. Maybe you aren't ready. Maybe movies aren't the best get-together for the two of you. But try it once, as practice, and see what happens. No matter how it goes, you're bound to learn something!

4

Rule Four: Know Yourself, Know Your Adversary

In the summer of 2023, my wife and I got run up on by the youth group from the First Church of White Christian Nationalism.

We were out at a public park, sitting on a bench and eating some excellent fried food. It's a big public square–type space— lots of families, kids on bikes, old guys on roller skates reliving their glory days of the '80s. All races, all generations, lots of working-class people. As an interracial, queer, working-class family, we appreciate this kind of space. My wife is a Black cis woman, I'm a White trans man, and we're both covered with tattoos, most of them religious. It's not always easy to blend in. So, that evening, we were happy to just be part of the crowd enjoying a summer evening by the water.

We're just digging into our takeout when a very young White man, maybe nineteen or twenty, suddenly gets on his portable sound system to try to save some sinners. He starts preaching into the microphone, and immediately, the crowd thins, the Friday night good vibes having been crushed. He carries on until park security rolls over in a golf cart to shut him down.

About then, I notice a small crowd of other young White men, probably ages fifteen to seventeen, coming to flank him defensively as the security guard speaks to him. As the security guard departs, I watch their group scan the crowd, smirking. Behind us, an older and fairly intoxicated gentleman gets on his own mic and starts karaoking in multiple languages. He's both excellent and funny as hell, breaking in with welcome commentary ("Don't you love it when twenty-year-olds come and try to tell grown-ass people how to live!")

I lose track of the group of young men for a moment, but minutes later, they're right next to me, asking my wife and I whether we know Jesus. I ignore them entirely, but my wife, being a better Christian than me, says yes. Their leader, the oldest one who had been on the mic, keeps pushing more questions: "Do you go to church? Is it a Bible-believing church? What's the name of the church? Where is it?"

It was all pushy, smug, and annoying as hell. Still, it was a pretty standard street proselytizing script—until he says, within inches of my wife's face, "It's not a Black Lives Matter church, is it?"

Immediately, I'm on my feet and in his face, ordering him to get back. Like clockwork, the rest of the Church Boy Brown Shirts swoop in to form a protective semicircle around him. I keep walking at him to force him to walk backward, repeating, "This is inappropriate, get back," loudly, over the top of him while he wheedles with a grin, "What's inappropriate? I'm just trying to talk about the Word of God! Did you know the Bible also says homosexuality is a sin?" The coordination of this entire event was so clear and so calculated. Clearly, these little assholes have been trained, coached, and released into the world by some White Christian national-ish church to test their mettle against the "ungodly."

I finally walk their lead boy far enough backward until they all peel off. My wife—ordained in two denominations, with a divinity degree from Harvard and a PhD from the School of Hard Knocks—is on her feet now too, itching to get at them.

We leave the park instead because their sole goal is provocation, because even negative attention feeds their hustle, because we have a movie to catch, and because we refuse to cede our date night to the Youth Group from Hell.

Wielding love and power

I have a biblical studies degree from an Ivy League institution, with a concentration in gender and sexuality in the New Testament. Back when I first got my degree, I thought it might serve me in situations like that one at the park—of which there have been many in my life, and no doubt there will be many more. But over time, I have learned that while studying the Bible as a text of liberation is incredibly valuable, these particular confrontations have nothing to do with Christian conversation, interpretation of Scripture, or a commitment to God. They have everything to do with power.

Power is the only language White Christian nationalism responds to. A liberatory interpretation of Scripture rooted in love only matters if it is leveraged by a movement with some kind of power. Policy analysis, policy proposals, policy enactment: these can only serve the ends of love when they are backed by power. Marching and demonstrations in defense of compassion and mercy are meaningless unless they are strategic displays of power, tied to a movement that will last after the streets are cleared. Dr. King said it best: "Power without love is reckless and abusive and . . . love without power is sentimental and anemic. Power at its best is love implementing the demands of justice. Justice at its best is love correcting everything that stands against love."

Whatever church got these baby-faced fascists hopped up on Gatorade and the art of publicly scapegoating Black and queer people did so in the service of building power. Young people are crucial to a movement's power; they are its longevity, its future leadership. The First Church of White Christian Nationalism takes this seriously. These White suburban hoodlums were trained to come out and not only recruit the willing but to publicly identify, target, and escalate the scapegoats. It takes very little to bridge the gap from generic toxic masculinity to weaponized imperial Christianity. All that kid had to do was sprinkle some Jesus words on top of his rabid entitlement and hate speech, and voilà: he's legally, culturally, and politically covered by the blood of Jesus and (according to White Christian nationalism's favorite legal defense) the First Amendment.

But guess what else?

These folks are powerful, yes. But they are not all-powerful. They'd like you to think that so you give up trying to push back. But they are outnumbered, and if we organize, we can use our numbers to outmaneuver them.

A righteous cleanup on aisle six

A few weeks after this incident in the park, my wife and I were in the grocery store and, bless the Lord, guess who we saw! The ringleader of the boy posse. He was alone and pushing his grocery cart, no minions to bolster his sense of owning the place.

My wife called to me, loudly, so the rest of the shoppers around us could hear, from the other side of the produce stand. "Is that who I think it is?!" she asked.

I called back, just as loud, "Oh yes, it is! That same little guy who ran up on us just to tell us that homosexuality is a sin! What a great approach!" At this point, all the other shoppers and store clerks are staring. The blood has drained from the little fella's face, and he's staring like a deer in the headlights, mumbling.

She says, "He said that, and he said that it goes against God to support Black Lives Matter. Well, look at this, this is nothing but God's work that we're both here again tonight. Because I need to tell you: you were wrong for that. That's not what the gospel says. And you need to know that he [she points to me] saved your life that night. Because he got to you first and pushed you away from me. If I had got you first—ooooooweee!"

He stammers something nonsensical and weak and continues to dig his own grave right there, between the onions and apples. "Black Lives Matter supports abortion," he mumbles. "I-I just want you to be saved."

At this wild twist in the conversation, the older Black woman restocking fruit bins next to us also whips around to stare him down, sliding her glasses down her nose like a grandma about to go off. My beautiful wife, always ready for it, brings her voice up a notch, "Oh, Black Lives Matter supports abortion;

THAT'S why you have a problem with it. Really? Well, Ms. Angela," she says, turning to the clerk at the fruit bins, reading her name tag. "I'm sorry, but you're about to have a cleanup situation on aisle six."

The clerk chuckles, smiles, and says, "Now, now." No one does anything to come to Teen Fascist's aid. He's alone in this space, he's shook up, he has recruited nobody, and he has been publicly marked as a bigot instead of a Nice White Christian Boy on at least two counts. He knows it, and the rest of the people in the produce department know it too. Our job is done; we roll out.

This is a small interaction in the grand scale of things. But it's going to take a lot of persistent, dogged vigilance in every space we can contend for to push White Christian nationalism back into the hole it crawled out of. It's going to require calling out White Christian nationalism in the produce aisle, in the streets, in the pews, and at the ballot box. To be clear: I'm not endorsing "callout culture" with this anecdote. Nor do I think the tactics of public shaming are always strategic when your target is someone who, though they may be wrong, has very little power. But when it comes to contending for public space and fighting spiritual malpractice and the brazen scapegoating of oppressed people, you have to check folks, and you have to check them immediately. You have to let them know that you also have power and that you are willing to use it.

We can't leave this at the one-on-one level, either. Little dude from the grocery store is not likely to hang up the megaphone after going one round in the produce department. And even if he did, there are countless others ready to take his place. What we need is our own mass movement truly contending for power to run the likes of this guy's older brother out of elected office, off the street corners, and out of their own pulpits (and yes, of course, ideally into our own movement for a thriving future for all people . . . once he's done hate-preaching at me and my wife on date night).

To really put the mass in mass movement, we gotta bring in every damn Randy and Brandy we can get. Again, there's just too many of them to ignore. And right now, that little street preacher is far more likely to have Randy and Brandy's recruitment on his to-do list than anyone else is. If we don't talk to them, guess who will?

Your future is Randy's present

I decided not to let that last rhetorical question hang in the air. The answer should be clear by now: if we don't talk to Randy, someone else will, and it might be that young street preacher. But it might also be the adults who are grooming that kid for leadership, who have seized control not just of many of the most influential and well-funded Christian institutions in the country but of the Republican Party, and through it, many of the national levers of power. And the thing is, these guys have gotten pretty damn good at talking to Randy, and they're getting better every day.

All my life, I have watched poor and working-class White folks around me—my family, my friends, most of the people I love—choke on White supremacy at the expense of our own liberation. A lot of the guys I came up with who bought into it most intensely are already dead before forty—from overdoses, suicide, and war. At the same time, all my life, I have also watched poor and working-class White folks around me—my family, my friends, most of the people I love—crack through the lie of White supremacy in our own lives. Sometimes it happens at work. Sometimes it happens in jail. Sometimes it happens in love. What's important is that it is literally happening all the time.

The hard truth is that, in large part, the progressive movement is not out there reaching for our people in this moment, despite the fact that escalating crises are driving more awakenings every day. While there have always been White people impacted by homelessness, police brutality, incarceration, and the drug economy, the levels at which Americans of all races—including White people—are being thrown into these conditions is speeding up at a pace probably not seen in the last century. Struggling White folks are already facing the reality that these issues are not "someone else's problem"; they're our problem too. But generally, there aren't progressive folks working to pull our communities into mass movements to contend with these issues. This kind of disregard for poor White folks by progressives isn't just cruel and wrong; it's also the express train to authoritarianism.

For fifty years, in every backwater hurt town that capital has fled and the Democratic Party has written off, White Christian nationalism has stepped into the vacuum of power. White Christian nationalism has been all too happy to bankroll demagogue politicians there, to misdirect regular-ass White people's legitimate fear and anger, and to set up churches and parachurch organizations to incubate the long-term work of building up bases, cadre, culture, property, and power.

As bad as all of that is, and as heavy as the weight of this country's history is when it comes to pitting us against Black and Brown people, poor White people in America still have the potential to be authoritarianism's Achilles heel. In 2019, there were over 140 million poor and low-income people in this country. And some 66 million of us were White. The vast majority of that 66 million are so stressed, pissed, overworked, and jaded that we don't vote. That's not because we don't care but because we don't see anybody who cares about us. This is what we have in common with all poor and oppressed people, across lines of race. We can unify the bottom to strike a blow at the top.

But somehow we're still falling woefully short at the task of unifying the bottom.

With friends like these, Randy doesn't need enemies

Don't overcomplicate this shit. We live in the richest country in the world—in the history of the world. But more than 140 million of us are living in poverty. These are not the conditions that breed a thriving democracy. Our economic and historic realities are precisely what give rise to the crises we're in. Criminalization of the poor is not separate from the erosion of democracy; criminalization of the poor *is* the erosion of democracy. Because people in jail can't vote. Health care denial, hunger, and poverty are not separate from voter suppression; health care denial, hunger, and poverty *are* voter suppression. Because dead people can't vote. This is why, when you've pledged allegiance to the bottom (which we'll look at in Rule Nine), you're less likely to be surprised by the future. It's not to say that poor people are magical oracles who can predict what's going to happen next Thursday (aside from a few talented, broke-ass clairvoyants I know). What I mean is that when you're poor like Randy— or really, when you belong to any disinherited or historically

marginalized group in America—odds are you have fewer illusions about what *civility, progress,* and even *democracy* mean. You
don't discount Trump or believe "he could never win," and you
are less surprised by events like J6.

Why? Because *civility* sounds like another universe when
you're at the Department of Social and Health Services, fighting
to keep your food stamps from being cut off. Because "progress"
means very little from the inside of a detention center. Because
in solitary confinement, "democracy" is something you might be
able to read about if you're extremely lucky, but you have already
been legally stripped of it. When you know America is already
pulling this kind of shit on millions of poor people, with those
numbers growing by the minute, it gets harder and harder to
buy the line "this could never happen in our great nation" that
captivates both conservatives and liberals. The worst has often
already happened to us.

Couple that with the inaccessibility of higher education
(only 37.7 percent of Americans have a bachelor's degree or
higher) and the woeful underinvestment of our public schools,
and you have a real spicy recipe for a nation of hurt folks who
are actively being kept from understanding the root causes of
our suffering.

Sure, it's possible that Randy simply enjoys loudmouthed,
ignorant bigotry; this is America after all, and bigotry is a classic
American pastime. But we cannot separate Randy's analysis from
the conditions he's living in. This whole damn country is set up
to keep poor people in the dark, shanking each other for scraps,
while the rich get richer.

Yet for all its overt White Christian nationalism in policy
and rhetoric, the Republican Party of today is doing a far better
job than the Democratic Party when it comes to superficially

marketing itself as the face of the multiracial (and even, to a degree, interfaith) working class. Sure, the deck is stacked in the far right's favor in some ways. Take, for example, the competing narratives between the Republican and Democratic parties.

The Republicans tell us: "Make America Great Again," which means it once was, and it sure as hell can be again if we make the right moves. Meanwhile, the Democrats say something like: "Trust us, the economy is strong (even though it doesn't feel that way), and we brought inflation down (even though things still cost a lot), and also racism is definitely bad and climate change is real, but we can't really do much about it. Oh, and the Republicans are killing our democracy, even though we can't tell you exactly what democracy is, other than the formal process of voting and elections . . . which, by the way, we are kindly asking you to donate to our campaign. Please, it couldn't be more urgent."

More deeply than this rhetorical imbalance, the conservative narrative strongly asserts that the great American imperial experiment is a historical triumph: it has been worth it, and it should continue unimpeded by demands for structural restitution of long-standing abuses, oppression, exploitation, genocidal violence, and mass impoverishment. This narrative is further bolstered by all kinds of American "common sense" sloganing that resonates in people's individual lives—the past is past; when life gives you lemons, make lemonade; to the victor go the spoils; survival of the fittest; etc. Scale all that talk up to the level of policy, of course, and you get something brutal and wrong. Still, it's clear and consistent AF.

The progressive narrative, conversely, can't seem to help itself when it comes to mealy-mouthed double-speak. Or even when the talk sounds good, it's all talk, no walk. "Cancel all student loan debt!" becomes "Cancel some student loan debt!" becomes "Cancel debts . . . only for the people least crushed by them!" becomes "Okay, we aren't actually canceling anything now." I can hear hundreds of progressives shutting down as I say this, because the truth hurts. But I'm gonna keep saying it for the handful of folks willing to face reality. The conservative movement in this country—at this late hour, as the sun is setting on what shreds of democracy ever existed here—is led by some truly brilliant demagogic motherfuckers, and they're running circles around their opposition.

If you want evidence of this, check out the *Mandate for Leadership 2025* from the Heritage Foundation, a conservative think tank that has had a hugely influential role on American conservatism since the Reagan era. This report was basically them doubling down on the bet that, with the 2024 election, their glory days were back. See the footnote below if you want to trip out on the full report.*

What's so sharp about this 920-page horror show? A few things:

1. It's anchored in the language of everyday values and framed in terms of the experiences of everyday Americans.
2. It's a politicizing how-to-manual for regular-ass people who don't understand the bajillion details of federal policy or the byzantine White House staff chain-of-command. It not only breaks down how various parts of

---

* You found it! Now proceed at your own risk: Heritage Foundation, *Mandate for Leadership 2025*, 2023, https://thf_media.s3.amazonaws. com/project2025/2025_MandateForLeadership_FULL.pdf.

government work at the federal level but also gives clear and accessible instruction on how a social movement should be influencing that government.

3. It makes use of theology in a way that bolsters its political arguments.

4. It speaks to the real suffering occurring across America, honestly acknowledging the likelihood that conditions of daily living are frightening and wholly unjust—poverty, violence, the addiction epidemic, deep inequality, the detachment of our political class from our dire everyday struggles—and then, through skillful sleight-of-hand, delivers both false diagnosis and false cure for these ills.

5. The scapegoating is tied directly to policy recommendations, giving it a horrifically efficient "let's-take-care-of-this-problem" vibe.

All of this underscores and complements the very effective strategies and tactics being run by White Christian nationalists right now. They've fully captured one of the major parties and, from that party capture, they've escalated toward full state capture. They've built their own media infrastructure. They cast a wide net across every little backwater church in Randyland a generation or two ago, and they left no stone unturned; no place was too small or too unimportant. They are also reaping the harvest they've sown in diverse recruitment, particularly through Black, Brown, and immigrant churches. It's not simply theology and funding that make that recruitment work: it's also a strong conservative framing for the real struggles facing these communities.

What's more, this agenda trickles down to local and state office and policies. There is a robust national network grooming local candidates, connecting them to a national network, and guiding White Christian nationalist politicians and leaders across the country to implement backwards-ass shit in their communities.

In June 2023, I found myself back in Washington D.C. with the Poor People's Campaign, this time for our Moral Poverty Action Congress, which included back-to-back days of political education, arts and culture, and over four hundred congressional visits, led by a multiracial legion of poor folks. Upon our group's departure from the D.C. Hilton (lesson #569 of poor people's organizing: take the nice bed and free shampoo when life offers it to you), we briefly overlapped in the hotel lobby with a huge incoming conference group full of delegations of Black and Latinx attendees. They were at least as diverse a crowd as the Poor People's Campaign's Moral Poverty Action Congress. We soon learned that they had turned out for the Faith & Freedom Coalition's Road to Majority conference, billed as "the nation's premiere pro-family and pro-faith event," including a presidential candidates' forum with the full cavalcade of White Christian nationalist candidates, from Mike Pence to Ron DeSantis to Trump himself. Highly notable was the fact that, along with the usual White Christian nationalist policy positions (abortion, marriage, Israel, and an unfettered free market), Faith & Freedom Coalition also lists immigration, justice reform, and "help for the poor, the needy, and those who have been left behind" as core among their issues and areas of work.

Now, did I see left-behind Randy in that hotel lobby, among that crowd? I did not! (Or, if he was there, one of the church ladies from the First Church of White Christian Nationalism had done a great job of stuffing him into an expensive suit and tie to cover up all his prison tattoos). You might think the place would've been full of Randys since I've been over here making the point that conservatives are getting better at selling salient narratives to the working class. And I think they are. But do they want to be seen with Randy in the halls of power? Hell no. They want to be seen with economically successful people. If anyone in their crew is telling a story about poverty, they better be telling a story about how hard work, prayer, and married parents helped them boot-strap their way out of it. You can't say private Christian charity is the best and only solution to poverty with some broke-ass sinner like Randy running around the joint, exposing the reality that private Christian charity wasn't enough to get him and the 140 million people in his shoes out of poverty![†]

It's this last bit that highlights for me how unfortunately similar Democrats' and Republicans' orientation to poor people is—not necessarily as a matter of policy but as a matter of orga-nizing. Leaders of both parties, I'm sure, would say that they're more caring and do more materially to help the poor than the other side.

But to center the realities, experiences, knowledge, leader-ship, and complex lives of living, breathing poor people is not in the interests of either side of America's ruling class. Why? Because whether you're talking to Randy in Randyland or poor people at the border, on the rez, in the projects—folks are going to let you know this system is not working for us and it never has, that it was never meant to, and that it's going to take a hell of a lot more than the smoke-and-mirrors of election season every four years to change that. Poor people must be heard. Not exploited. Not silenced. Not pimped for our sad stories and street credibility. Heard.

---

† I did, however, see Randy and several of our cousins at the Poor Peo-ple's Congress, studying policy and economics for three days straight, among a multiracial coalition of the poor.

And most importantly, we must be answered to.

So how do you get heard when you're poor in America?

You get a big goddamn gang, that's how.

A movement-sized gang.

A gang with room for every size, shape, and stripe of broke, pissed, and hungry.

A gang that stretches all the way, as we say in the Poor People's Campaign, from the hood to the holler.

Sounds ambitious, and it is. But not impossible. It's happened more than once in history, more than once in America. This is the kryptonite of White Christian nationalism and of imperialism itself, both of which hinge so completely on the strategy of divide and conquer.

Exercise: Study your local opponents

I don't know where you live, but if you live in America today, you're probably not too far from a White Christian nationalist holding a position of elected office. Choose the nearest one, or maybe just the one that grinds your gears the most. It could be a school board member, a county commissioner, a mayor—take your pick. Read up on their campaigns and policies, read their candidate statements and interviews, watch their ads, comb through their websites. Then answer the following questions:

1. Who funded this person's campaign? What and who else do they fund?
2. How does this person frame the problems facing your community? Which parts of this frame are accurate? Which parts are misleading?

3. Why did this person resonate with enough people in your community to win their election?
4. What would it take to effectively counter this person's campaign next time around?
5. What would it take to effectively shift Randy away from supporting this candidate?

5

Rule Five: Calculate Your Risks

In June 2020, on the streets of the small town of Aberdeen, Washington, I was hemmed in by a large, heavily armed crowd of (mostly) White men. The "Back the Blue" counterprotestors were spitting, screaming slurs, and rushing toward me with their loaded guns pointed. Several were drunk.

The most worked-up of the bunch carried an open tallboy of Rolling Rock in his back pocket. He nearly fell on top of his own assault rifle multiple times. And though absolutely nobody was pointing a weapon back at him, he sported a tactical vest. A few of his compatriots wore militia insignia—although they could not be described as "well regulated," as the Second Amendment reads, by any stretch of the imagination.

All of this happened because I had helped to organize a small candlelight vigil for local people—most of them homeless, nearly all of them disabled—who had died at the hands of law enforcement in recent years. We had coordinated the timing of our vigil to show our support for the families and communities of Breonna Taylor and George Floyd. Our small vigil was one of countless protests against police brutality and anti-Blackness taking place all over the world. The global uprising for racial justice had come to our small town, and our team was eager to be part of it.

The victims of police brutality in our majority-White region of the country were both White and Indigenous—and, in such a small place, known personally by vigil attendees and counter-protestors alike. So, it was clear that this was not an abstract, "out-there" issue only hurting someone else's neighborhood. This was an Aberdeen issue too.

We knew there was a buildup of misinformation leading up to our vigil, such as the Facebook rumor that "antifa" was coming to town to loot local businesses. We proceeded anyway. We had held similar vigils each year for the previous five years, and each had elicited the same rumors and victim-blaming. Those prior vigils had usually drawn one open-carrying counterprotester and a salty cop or two, but with little more drama than that. What was most important to us, as always, was that those who had died unjustly—because they were poor, homeless, disabled, criminalized—had a space to be remembered publicly by those who loved them.

The clearest divide between the vigil participants and the counterprotestors that day was, in fact, not race, region, or religion. Most of the crowd, on both sides, was White—although it needs to be said that the one Black woman in the vigil crowd was stalked, harassed, and threatened by counterprotestors for weeks afterward. Just about everyone on both sides came from the same small, rural county. The religious mix on both sides was similar, with a pretty even number of Christians in both groups. The sharpest distinction between the two groups, by far, was where their class sympathies lay.

Those who had turned out for the vigil—friends and family members of victims of police brutality—were poorer. Many were currently or formerly homeless. Many had experienced incarceration; even if they had wanted to, they would have been unable to acquire a firearm due to their criminal records.

That same prohibition was clearly not shared by the counter-protest camp. The wealthiest can always keep their hands clean by outsourcing the dirty work of legal violence or extralegal vigilantism. Those they often outsource it to are petit-bourgeoise conservatives, as was the case that day. It was mainly small-business owners (or those aspiring to be so) who chased us from street corner to street corner that day, alternately brandishing weapons and taking photos with the police.

Their threat of physical violence was matched by their dehumanizing language; on top of every imaginable racial, gendered, and homophobic slur came a constant barrage of specific, personal attacks on people who struggled with homelessness and addiction: "Yeah, I knew your brother," one man yelled at someone in our group. "I know everything that happened the day the police shot him. He was a junkie, he deserved to die."

I am not responsible for the reckless and violent decisions made by counterprotesters that day. But I still feel angry with myself for underestimating the backlash we walked into. Because of my work in street and jail outreach, I was plugged into the reality that life for poor people in America in 2020 was as bad as ever. I knew we were doing human rights organizing in a mean little town. I knew the town's long history of vigilante violence against poor and homeless people, from the heyday of the Industrial Workers of the World's free speech strikes to the present. Our planning team for the vigil and our group of local clergy had already been subject to public death threats more than once over the past decade, with absolutely no response from local police.

Still, that day, a mob of men drew their guns on a crowd of completely unarmed demonstrators, mainly women and several children, in broad daylight. This was a significantly new level of risk, even for us.

I've taken stock of that day frequently during recent years. And I've wondered why the level of threat and violence still managed to take me by surprise.

What had shifted? What form is White Christian nationalism taking now, and what form is it likely to take in the future? What risks will it present as it shifts and changes shape? How will we discern what risks we are willing to take in the future, and how will we weigh those risks against our calling to struggle for justice?

Reading the future

In the immediate aftermath of that vigil and the gun-toting counterprotestors that it drew, I began to understand that the decision to connect our local struggles as poor people—in our case, poor Whites and poor Indigenous people—to the struggles of Black people across the US drew far more backlash than usual. Poor Whites in this country have long been incentivized to turn our backs on poor people of every other race. Breaking out of that script comes with consequences.

The team that planned the vigil included several younger White men recovering from addiction who were involved in recovery groups. I learned from them that many recovery networks were being increasingly propagandized by far-right White nationalist networks. Indeed, some of the key organizers and agitators for the racist counterprotest that day were sponsors in AA and NA and had turned out their group members to the event.

When I look back on that vigil a couple years later, it now seems clear to me that White Christian nationalist networks all over the country spent the year leading up to 2020 staging warm-up events for January 6. Unfortunately, ours happened to be one of these. Suffice to say, when January 6 itself finally came, it was hard for many of us to muster much surprise. Like I said before, when you're on the ground in a community where democracy has already been pretty roughed up, you sort of expect it to happen again, somewhere else, bigger and bolder.

It's okay to shut up, go home, and stay alive

At this point you may be thinking, "This guy doesn't sound like he was very successful at counter-recruiting anybody from White Christian nationalism that day." Nope, I sure wasn't. I didn't walk up to the drunk guy waving his assault rifle and say, "Let me show you a better way, brother!"

Here's something valuable to remember about counter-recruitment: it's not the right tactic for every situation. Even for multiple people navigating the same situation, each person is gonna face a different level of risk based on a whole constellation of factors. I remember my mentor, Willie Baptist, telling me about a march for universal health care he helped lead across the state of Pennsylvania in the 1990s. Somewhere in Pennsyltucky, a White militia came out to meet them—so the marchers sent their White organizers out to parlay. Then, as their march got closer to Philadelphia, the Nation of Islam came out, and the marchers sent their Black organizers to meet them. Read the room; you won't ever regret it.

There are going to be times, places, and people with whom your only option is to minimize your risk of being physically harmed. Do not engage in a political and theological debate with someone who is pointing a weapon at you. Just get yourself and your people the hell out of there.

This was particularly challenging on that sunny June afternoon in 2020. I was in the company of some of the bravest, kindest, and scrappiest people I know—folks who were appalled at the idea that we might simply walk away and not engage with self-deputized drunks who were screaming insults about our beloved dead. My coworker (we'll call her Candy), a former biker with a strict code of conduct for street etiquette, was outraged by the cowardice of grown-ass men chasing an unarmed peaceful crowd of mostly women. She could not help herself and hollered at one of them, "Sorry your dick's so small!" The man's face fell—she had clearly hit close to home—and he briefly disappeared in the crowd to recover. A few minutes later, he resurfaced and yelled, "Who said that! I'll whip it out right here and prove you wrong!" To which she calmly replied, without even pausing, "Sorry, I didn't bring my glasses with me."

I love Candy's heart and her courage so much. But if ever there should have been a day without dick jokes, this was it. Thankfully, the guys with the guns didn't decide right then and there to pop off. If they had, the story would have ended up very differently.

You don't show up to a gunfight with a prayer candle and then stick around and argue with your opponent. Jesus's words in Matthew 10:16 seem apt here: "See, I am sending you out like sheep into the midst of wolves, so be wise as serpents and innocent as doves." If White Christian nationalism is a cult of social and political violence, sign me up for whatever cult is committed to the prevention of senseless death. We already have enough martyrs to last us into the next millennia.

Your people are your safety

Your personal risk calculations cannot be made in a vacuum. While it's supremely helpful to gather as much information as you can about navigating your local terrain, keeping the big picture in mind is always key:

1. White Christian nationalist networks are better funded than you and I are.
2. White Christian nationalist networks are better organized than you and I are.
3. White Christian nationalist networks have robustly outgunned you and me.

"What the hell do we have to work with, then?" you may be wondering.

Well, we lucky ducks have the chaotic, messy, unorganized masses of regular-ass people. And prayer. We're going to need the constant assistance of both—especially when it comes to navigating issues of risk and safety.

I know this is a hard sell. Stay with me.

The illusion of safety is a delusion that will only put you and those you love in greater danger.

Now, it is true that once you clearly identify yourself, through action, as a person seeking to counter White Christian nationalism, then yes, those crosshairs are going to become a little more singularly focused on you. And if you happen to do a particularly good job—if you hit a weak spot in the story White Christian nationalism likes to tell about the world, for example, or if you are effective in building up a little bit of people power to shift a local election—those crosshairs get even tighter on your back. It's important to know this and take it seriously.

So, as you are thinking about how you want to pitch in and make your contribution, it's also important to think through things like:

* Who are people in my circle I know I can deeply trust, especially in a crisis?
* Who are people in my circle I'm connected to but can't necessarily trust in a crisis?
* Do I have a home safety plan for myself and my family?
* Where can I and/or my family go if we need to leave town for a few days?
* What's my phone tree of people to alert when I learn there's an unsafe situation unfolding?
* Some elements of getting through an unsafe situation require public exposure, but other elements require confidentiality. What's an example of each? How might I navigate both of these safety needs?

Nobody else can answer these questions for you, so your assignment for this chapter is to answer them for yourself. If you need to discuss elements of these questions with your family, loved ones, or emergency contacts, make sure you do so. It can feel scary to think through this stuff explicitly, so keep in mind that ideally, you will never need to refer to these plans. Ideally, you will never need the smoke alarms installed in your home either. But right now, White Christian nationalism is out here busier than a firebug in a drought-struck forest.

As you think through your own personal risks, don't lose sight of the bigger picture. This might all sound a little too grassroots and too small-scale. On one hand, it is. Why? Because while White Christian nationalism has been steadfastly building out its massive grassroots reach for decades, the rest of us haven't kept pace. We either didn't have the resources to do so or didn't realize just how rapidly and efficiently White Christian nationalism was scaling up its threat level, or some combination of the two. Either way, at this point, we need to build from the literal ground up, and no one and no place is unimportant or insignificant in this effort.

On the other hand, regular, struggling people are incredibly powerful when we come together. I know it's hard to feel that way in this country. The forces bolstering White Christian nationalism thrive off our sense of isolation and powerlessness, and they are more than happy to reinforce those feelings at every turn, to their immense benefit.

But we are neither isolated nor powerless. In the words of Rev. Dr. Martin Luther King Jr.: "There are millions of poor people in this country who have very little, or even nothing, to lose. If they can be helped to take action together, they will do so with a freedom and a power that will be a new and unsettling force in our complacent national life."

If you picked up this book because you are a regular person who wants to do your part to make this country a place less wracked by White Christian nationalist violence, then you are one of the millions of people Dr. King was talking about. Do not forget that you are worth protecting, just as you seek to protect others. White Christian nationalism is nihilistic enough, and quite possibly the best counter to nihilism is proactively keeping yourself and others alive and well.

So proceed with equal amounts of courage and caution. You're gonna need a lot of both.

Exercise: Calculate your own risks

After you answer the above questions, run through some worst-case scenarios. You can borrow details from any number of headlines where White Christian nationalists are dangerously running amok. Try to put yourself in the shoes of a regular person on the ground who happened to be in one of those headline stories and ask:

* Do you see people responding in ways that are truly helpful?
* Do you see people responding in ways that might be well-intentioned but end up making things even more dangerous, especially for vulnerable people?
* Were any weaknesses or contradictions of White Christian nationalism exposed in this moment?
* How might White Christian nationalists use this moment—even if it's a tragedy—to bolster their position?

✻ How can I navigate this situation both safely and strategically (such as managing risks while not playing into
the hands of White Christian nationalists, not giving
White Christian nationalists a bunch of media time
they can manipulate to their liking)?

Write down your answers. If you are already part of a community
having conversations about these things (a church, a community
group, an activist organizing group), talk through these questions and your responses together.

Finally, follow up with an exercise in brainstorming how to
proactively build safety with lots of other people before crisis
hits. The best defense is a good offense—a rule that White
Christian nationalism certainly practices in its own demagogic
way. But just because they're demagogues doesn't mean they get
to corner the market on good strategy. There are good people all
around you in your community. They probably think differently
about lots of stuff than you do. But they also probably have a
lot of things in common with you, especially when it comes
to facing a crisis. And whether you're planning for worst-case
tragedy scenarios or fending off an autocrat running for mayor,
White Christian nationalism presents us with lots of crises to
navigate.

Start thinking about the ways you're connected to people in
your sphere of influence and what you might have in common
with them: coworkers, neighbors, people who shop or work at
the grocery store you go to. Start noticing all the little chances
you have to deepen your connection with them and start to
build those relationships. Why? Because, again, all we have on
our side is people. Regular people. And it's impossible to be safe
or strategic when you're isolated from the people around you. As

you deepen these everyday connections, start to also analyze the regular, everyday world around you:

* Where are people most vulnerable to the worst threats of White Christian nationalism where you live? Is it shoppers at grocery stores in racially segregated neighborhoods? Transgender public school students who are under attack via policy from local school board candidates? Unhoused people subject to vigilante harassment and "bum bashing?" White teenage boys being profiled and targeted for online radicalization and recruitment? Identify the three groups of people you have some connection to in your everyday life—such as location, voting district, church, or neighborhood—who are most vulnerable to the attacks or enticements of White Christian nationalism.

* What might one effective, meaningful, and long-lasting intervention look like to lessen the threat of White Christian nationalism in these spaces?

* Is there a role you could play in this intervention? If not, who would be effective in this role?

Is someone in your community already working this angle? What support might they need? What meaningful contribution could you make to the work already being done (i.e., volunteer time)?

6

Rule Six: Get a
Religious Strategy,
Even If You Aren't Religious

Let me be real clear: you don't need to be religious, or Christian, or have a personal relationship with Jesus Christ to effectively counter White Christian nationalism. Certainly, it helps to know a little bit about the Man from Galilee in order to understand that White Christian nationalists are, by and large, lying their asses off about him. If you are a Christian, or a Christ follower, or a believer, or whatever you call yourself, then sure, you're a unique asset in this movement. But you don't need to ride for Team Jesus in Your Heart in order to help turn this shit around.

Here's something you might need, though.

Whatever your religious or spiritual practice is—whatever habits, rituals, and relationships keep you anchored in your deepest values of justice for all people—hold tight and go deeper with those. Doesn't matter if it's prayer, meditation, talking to your tomato plants, weightlifting, or spending time with your grandma. Do what you have to do to stay rooted in a clear and compelling sense of what's real, what's right, and who you are in the middle of it all.

Why? Because we ain't seen nothing yet. Anyone who wants in on countering this shit has got to have the grounding, the stamina, the clarity, and the motivation to face a worsening situation.

January 6, as I said before, wasn't the main act; it was the warm-up. White Christian nationalism is wholly undeterred in this moment. We have to move forward with this understanding. The powers-that-be behind White Christian nationalism are using every escalating crisis they encounter as an opportunity to continue building their base, their platforms, and their power. And unless you're living under a rock or on a yacht, you know there's no shortage of crises to choose from.

Will lighting candles and chanting prayers or mantras stall or beat back White Christian nationalism's ascendance? Hell no, it will not. But if lighting candles and chanting gets you in a better frame of mind to honestly assess the world around you, tap into a sense of deep collective belonging and responsibility, and harness your personal power to do something about the fuckery of White Christian nationalism, then by all means, light 'em up! Anchor down in your own spiritual strength, whatever it is.

Special shout-out at this point to any readers personally averse to Christianity who have made it this far in the book. You've been hanging tough through all the Jesusy noise. I see you and admire your discipline. Consider it all part of your Randy-whisperer workout regimen. Anyway, I'm super glad you're reading this. You have an important and unique role to play in countering White Christian nationalism in this country. Yes, I talk about Jesus, the Bible, and church many times throughout this book (kind of hard to avoid when you're a second-generation preacher writing about White Christian nationalism). The reasons for this are two-prong.

First, all these powerful people working overtime to make America even more exclusionary and bigoted, while claiming to follow a brown-skinned Palestinian Jew who was executed for building a poor people's movement and giving away free food and health care to anyone who wants it?! Well, it boils my grits, and something needs to be said about the hypocrisy.

Second, this goes far beyond just grinding my own personal axe. It's a matter of strategy.

Indeed, White Christian nationalists are hella suspect when it comes to giving a damn about anything Jesus actually said or did. But they are highly strategic when it comes to navigating the mental terrain of many regular-ass American people. They understand that we're all carrying around a lifetime of program-ming (call it "social conditioning," "brainwashing," whatever) that often causes us to make certain associations, assumptions, and conclusions, regardless of reality, history, or our own best interests.

Example: remember that song "God Bless the U.S.A.?" When I was a kid, I believed this was hands down the greatest song ever written. Why? Because it was dramatic. It talked about "the men who died"—for me, personally! It had that military snare beat in the background. Most importantly, when I sang it, the lyrics made it a song about me being proud of myself, for having been arbitrarily born in a particular geographic location at an arbitrary era in human history.

Sure, when I watch the music video today as a grown-ass man (quick recap: a farmer guy is literally evicted, and the video ends with him shuffling off under a damn "public auction" sign), I ask myself, "Why, in the year of our lord 1984, were all these White people sitting around a dinner table dressed for *Little House on the Prairie*? And more importantly, why are they all eating and singing together to celebrate when this poor dude apparently just lost his farm to a foreclosure?" The answer is that this music video was a greatest-hits compilation of 1980s "real American" symbols: tractors, cowboy hats, veterans in uniform, a turkey dinner, women in aprons. And most importantly, everyone in the whole dang video is White and holding hands in prayer. The story told in the video is of a hardworking White man with a wife and children who loses his farm to foreclosure and is fed and prayed with by his neighbors and family. It succinctly communicates the Reaganomic values of that era: when times are hard, don't complain or come looking to the government for help. Just go eat a lavish old-fashioned turkey dinner at your neighbor's house, look at black-and-white family photo albums together, then pack up the truck and bootstrap your way out of it.

The point of stuff like this is never to accurately portray America as it was, is, or will be. The point is to tug on people's imaginations and emotions. I don't care how scientifically minded, cynical, and self-preserving you are; we're all walking around with tuggable stuff rattling around inside our brains and hearts. Religion factors powerfully into this rattling for many people, in part because it saturates so much of our history.

Religion also connects, for better or worse, with the deepest parts of life: birth, death, grief, joy, hardship, community, family, sacrifice, morality, the whole nine yards. Religion, in this sense, goes far beyond what you as an individual believe or where you worship. It's a bigger social backdrop than one particular creed and holy text.

Think again about that "God Bless the U.S.A." video. For all the God name-dropping, the repeated images of prayer, and the undoubted assumption we're meant to make about the religious identity of these nice White Americans at the dinner table, there's nothing particularly Christian here. This is not a song about worshiping Jesus. This is a song about worshiping America—specifically, the American flag and the American military. Not much of a coincidence or accident, then, that popularity of this song surged during the first Gulf War.

Even as they double down on their (highly selective) Bible thumping and church growing, White Christian nationalists have been cashing in on this kind of broad and diffuse *relig-ish* stuff for decades. This whole aesthetic gives a superficial, Christian-y cultural cover for White Christian nationalist values, practices, and policies, which is a pretty strategic way to distract people when those values, practices, and policies happen to be in direct conflict with the words of their own messiah.

Right now, through White Christian nationalism, we are seeing a social movement using the power of religion for the worse. It is unfolding before our eyes daily. We have watched a religious-political movement fully capture one of two major parties with minimal resistance, and we are now on our way to witnessing full state capture. White Christian nationalists don't believe in the Bible unless it's propping up their status, power, and control over other people.

So what the hell does bad 80s music have to do with us trying to counter White Christian nationalism? No matter how confused or amused that video makes you, you've got to admit, it taps into the power of religion to change hearts and minds. What if we could tap into the power of religion for different ends? What if we were able, through our organizing, to tap into people's deepest beliefs and values not for the sake of propping up imperialism's divide and conquer but for the sake of uniting the bottom—across all lines of division—to transform centuries of injustice and harm?

We deserve to live

Can we imagine what it looks like for religion and spirituality to play a role in countering this movement? Not as a pious, one-person protest shouting down the MAGA camp but something powerful enough and collective enough to make a difference? We have plenty of examples from history, but what would it look like today? Could you imagine a spiritually anchored mass liberation movement so strong and effective it captures a major party—or births a new, truly viable third party of poor and struggling people—and forces policy positions that actually adequately address the crises of poverty, climate change, systemic racism, gender-based violence, ableism, homelessness, incarceration, and more?

Having a religious strategy doesn't mean you personally need to become religious. What it means is that you understand the pivotal role religion has played in social movements throughout US history. It means you don't write all religious communities off as inherently irrelevant (though some may be) or inherently oppressive (though some certainly are). It means you study the way White Christian nationalists distort religion to further their political project, and you understand the strategic value of exposing this distortion.

First of all, we have to be with folks at the bottom. Second, we have to speak and move with people in a way that resonates more deeply than White Christian nationalism. If White Christian nationalism is seeking to exploit people's fear and anger through misdirection and religious scapegoating—which it is—then we have to be able to help people aim that fear and anger at the systems and policies (for you churchy types, the "powers and principalities") actually responsible for regular people's suffering. And we have to disrupt the religious scapegoating.

We cannot do this simply by indiscriminately shitting on people of faith.

I say all of this because much of progressive organizing in this country won't go near religion or spirituality with a ten-foot pole (by "religion" here, I mean formal, organized belief systems and institutions, and by "spirituality," I mean sacred experiences, encounters, and rituals that exist both within and outside of religion). And I get that. I understand that a lot of people who have found their way toward progressivism have often pointed themselves in that direction in the first place because they've been deeply hurt and traumatized by religion in the form of The First Church of White Christian Nationalism. I get that religious trauma can put a hurting on your ability to trust the potential power and intelligence of collective spiritual practice when most of what you've personally experienced is spiritual malpractice.

But let's be clear about something: White Christian nationalism does not have a corner on the market of spirituality, religion, morality, Christianity, or even God's own self. The very fact that White Christian nationalists want you to believe that they are the only "real" Christians should tell you just how powerful of a role religion plays in the service of social movements.

This is not about having a "gotcha!" approach either, just so you can feel smug and self-satisfied in understanding the power of religion better than White Christian nationalists do. They don't give a rat's ass about your smugness or self-satisfaction. They care about power, and they have it. If we don't have it, we clearly don't understand the power of religion better than they do.

That's not at all to say that White Christian nationalists are doing a better job at following Jesus simply because their power is ascendant. What I'm saying is that they understand the role that faith and spirituality can play in the lives of millions of regular, hurting people, and they've figured out how to exploit this to the benefit of their political movement. If we want to effectively counter White Christian nationalism, we need to likewise understand the role that faith and spirituality can play in the lives of millions of regular, hurting people—and figure out how to leverage this for the sake of justice.

This isn't crazy talk. This is US history. Ministers and evangelists ran the Underground Railroad. The Civil Rights Movement was incubated in church basements. For every genocidal religious zealot in American history, there are just as many faithful people who, because of their moral code and spiritual training, have stood against injustice. Spirituality is important for social movements because it lasts longer than a damn campaign cycle, because it can anchor masses of people in critical day-to-day spade work even when nobody's paying them to do it, and because it can build resilience in the face of crisis and loss. Human beings are not disembodied heads interested in endless, obsessive analysis over the latest polling data. We look at the

world around us with human eyes. We look for human relationships. We look for community.

Now, what would it take to pull enough people into that
movement that it's strong enough to take power? And what
would it take to get them to stick and stay through generations
of rebuilding our whole society from the bottom up?

We actually have the beginnings of one already, scattered
across thousands of hard-up neighborhoods across the country.
This extremely grassroots but deeply relational network is teth-
ered by small but powerful groups doing the work of holding
down their communities regardless of all the storms that come:
Chaplains on the Harbor, Set It Off Movement, the National
Union of the Homeless, the General Baker Institute, Greater
Birmingham Ministries, the Coalition of Immokalee Workers,
the Rural Organizing Project, Union de Vecinos, Put People
First! PA, and countless powerful local networks coming together
to organize the bottom not only through campaign-style work
but also through arts, culture, projects of survival, healing, deep
community building, and spiritual care.

Something you gotta understand about poor people's organizing is that it's spiritual. Death stalks constantly. We as poor
people are in touch with our mortality. We as poor people are
forced to see the stark truth behind so many hypocrisies propping up this society. We as poor people survive on the joyful grit
and militant tenderness that keeps us finding beauty, laughter,
and lifelines amid the wreckage of daily apocalypses.

Being spiritual doesn't mean poor people trust religious institutions or even God. But the detached, dry, jargony, academic
culture most progressives inhabit also falls damn short of trust-
worthiness. Spirituality is not just an idea or a theory. Nor is
spirituality a warm, comforting feeling.

Spirituality is your hungry, grieving, dopesick body and mind deciding together to get up and live another day.

Faith is deciding that you deserve life when the powers and principalities of this world tell you every fucking second of every day that you do not.

Religion is a moral code, a moral habit that sits deeper in you than all your other habits, and by this definition of it, a lot of poor folks put nice, respectable-looking church people to shame. How? I can't tell you the number of times I've watched other poor people spend their literal last dime to help someone "who needed it more." I haven't ever actually seen comfortable church folks do this.

Hope is not optimism. Hope is something we have to go out and build, in concrete and material ways. Hope is food. Hope is sanctuary. Hope is Narcan. Hope, for poor people, is inseparable from life and inseparable from power.

Spirituality is the stuff that allows us to be tough as nails when protecting our lives and our people, and more tender than the tiny first green shoots of spring when we're cradling the fragile, radical hope of a new generation. Because despite this hellish system's best efforts, despite all of us it killed, some of us are still here, and we live on for all of us.

Spirituality and spiritual communal care are an indispensable part of what it will take to support and sustain that leadership from the bottom of society. Some of this looks like "projects of survival"–style organizing: taking spaces like a free, welcoming, and nonjudgmental community lunch program and intentionally seeding them with conversations and education on systemic injustice, history, and political economy. People are just as hungry to be treated as thinkers and leaders as they are hungry for a hot meal. You can do this in ways that are accessible to a whole range of people instead of clobbering people over the head with the latest hot political book you read. At Chaplains on the Harbor, we did it with the art and posters we put up on the wall, in the conversations we struck up while scrubbing out toilets at the shelter, and with the way we held meetings to ensure full participation was possible for folks who couldn't read.

Some of this spiritual communal care looks like carving out the ritual spaces for poor people to mark the value and dignity of our own lives—to do our own people's funerals, weddings, and baptisms when most other religious institutions are inaccessible or scapegoating us, when the state is breaking our families apart, and when we cannot afford the cost of our own burials or cremations. On the Harbor, we crowdfunded many funerals. We baptized babies for parents just before their families were separated by CPS. We also held some of the most tender weddings. We got cakes decorated to celebrate everything: "Welcome Home from Jail!" "Congrats on Finishing Probation!" "You Did It, Drug Court Graduate!" When this world is stingy with luck and fortune, you have to go the extra mile to claim your joy and celebrate your people.

There are churches out there literally preaching that our people deserve to die—because we're felons, because we're junkies, because we're homeless, because we're trailer trash, because we're not saved. We can't just counter that idea by saying, "Well, only dummies believe in God," or "Religious people are just wishful thinkers." We can't counter with a response that skips over religion altogether.

Whether we as individuals are religious or not, all faith traditions, including Christianity, stand in judgment of people abusing their power—especially those who abuse it in order to keep our people dying from health care denial, freezing to death on the street, or being killed at the hands of law enforcement. We have to preach that our people deserve to live.

Reading the Bible with Randy in mind

Some of this spiritual communal care entails doing deep excavating of our values to see whether they really are anchored in love, truth, and justice or whether they've been compromised by White Christian nationalist influence. There is a range of ways to do this, as varied as the innumerable faith and community groups that are doing it.

One way that I've found incredibly helpful is to approach holy texts with the primary orientation of our people's liberation. Organizers of all religious and spiritual backgrounds have done work with sacred texts of many traditions, with many powerful results across human history. The particular stretch of human history closest to mine and Randy's neck of the woods happens to be twenty-first-century America, where the Bible is still the bestselling book of all time, so that's the text I'm using for this chapter. At the Kairos Center, where I was trained, we call this "reading the Bible with the poor."

Sometimes, reading the Bible with the poor might mean, yes, literally sitting down and reading Scripture in the company of organized poor folks and listening for the resonance in conditions, experiences, and insights across millennia, with an intentional eye to the economic backdrop of each story. But you can also do this in other contexts if you bring the right lens. It changes just about everything when you begin looking for poor people every time you turn the page in the Bible. And it just so happens that poor people are there. From the Israelites going toe to toe with Pharaoh, to the prophets decrying the abuses of the wealthy, to baby Jesus being born into a refugee family on the run across the border, to parables like widow and the unjust judge, to the entire Epistle of James. . . . You can't get around us. That's the history we inherit.

And who knows, maybe it's too optimistic of me to think that you're going to sit down with Randy and read the Bible together. Ideally, you'll find a community where you can do that—read a sacred text with someone from Randy's world. If you can't do that, you could at least try to read a passage from Scripture looking for the power of poor folks within it.

Here's an example of how it looks to read the Bible with the poor. Let's look at Luke 18:9–14:

> Jesus told this parable to some who trusted in themselves that they were righteous and regarded others with contempt: "Two men went up to the temple to pray, one a Pharisee and the other a tax collector. The Pharisee, standing by himself, was praying thus, 'God, I thank you that I am not like other people: thieves, rogues, adulterers, or even like this tax collector. I fast twice a week; I give a tenth of all my income.' But the tax collector, standing far off, would not even look up to heaven, but was beating his breast and saying, 'God, be merciful to me, a sinner!' I tell you, this man went down to his home justified rather than the other; for all who exalt themselves will be humbled, but all who humble themselves will be exalted."

Who do we picture when we see this tax collector? Do we imagine an old-timey IRS employee of the Bible days, dressed for the office? Someone who, though he may not be respected, is at least considered respectable? It's hard to translate this line of work across the millennia. It's hard to capture how thoroughly despised—and neither respected nor respectable—tax collectors were when Jesus walked the earth. When we read "tax collector" in this scripture, we should not picture an IRS agent. It would be truer to history to imagine the tax collector as someone like a drug dealer.

Tax collectors, in this time and place, had dangerous and insecure jobs. They carried out some of the dirtiest work of the Roman Empire—not because of their strong moral allegiance to the empire but because they got paid for it. As a means of surviving in a chaotic and brutal economy, they often further corrupted the already-corrupt duties assigned them: by taking an extra cut for themselves on top of the taxes they were collecting. Any money they made for themselves they probably stole. They were seen, for many legitimate reasons, as collaborators in the destruction of their own struggling, occupied communities.

Tax collectors were not government employees; they were individual contractors. They were not on top of the pyramid scheme of Roman taxation; they were not even in the middle. Those of the same rank as the disciple Matthew and the tax collector of this parable were slaves or people from the lower class hired out for this work. Because of their contact with the Romans, they were stigmatized as "unclean." Socially, they were ranked with murderers and robbers. Their testimonies were not accepted in Judean courts, they were not eligible for Judean charity, and they were not even permitted to change their funds at the treasury.

It makes sense, on one level, for Judean society and the Pharisee to identify this group as "the problem." The sins of the tax collectors were visible. Struggling Galilean farmers could see the tax collectors stopping them at the entrances to cities, pawing through their crops and goods, always taking more than was honest, more than the peasants could afford to part with. Less visible were those middlemen the tax collectors worked for. Less visible still: the senators and magistrates who were explicitly and by law "prohibited from engaging in business or trade" themselves but were directly enriched by the taxation system. They made sure that the economic violence keeping their entire system afloat was outsourced to poor and desperate people.

In Grays Harbor County, the street drug economy is a major employer. It has become a primary replacement economy since the timber industry went abroad, and it operates in tandem with the industry of incarceration, the lucrative business of keeping jails and prisons full. I know and love many drug dealers. Most of the drug dealers I know are concerned with buying food for themselves or their children and with paying rent (if they're lucky enough to have housing at all). Most of the drug dealers I know are people who cannot secure living-wage employment through any legal means. Because of criminal records and outstanding warrants, I know many people involved in the drug economy who—like the tax collectors—are unable to access the social safety net. I know drug economy workers who have been denied health care after being profiled as IV drug users. I know at least one young man who died from this form of health care denial— and just like the tax collectors, the testimony of his friends was not accepted in the investigation of his death because they, too, were involved in the drug economy.

Yet despite these systemic cruelties, most of the drug dealers I know tend to be far more personally ashamed of the role they've had to play in surviving this economy—far more ashamed than the hospital administrators, far more ashamed than those holding the purse strings of the social safety net, far more ashamed than any elected officials or clergy. And certainly far and away more ashamed than the CEOs and founding families of pharmaceutical companies who continue to make money hand over fist from manufacturing the opioid epidemic.

Why does Jesus cast down the Pharisee and lift up the dealer in this parable? Not for abstract metaphysical reasons. Jesus's morality is always as material as it is spiritual. When the Pharisee calls himself pious, he lies. He fasts and tithes vigilantly, but what is this worth if he still identifies poor and stigmatized people as the enemies of righteousness? It's akin to praying, "God, I thank you that I am not like other people: gang members, prisoners, sex workers, or even like this drug dealer. I only buy organic fair-trade food, and I write a monthly check to my favorite nonprofit."

Jesus is not having it with that prayer!

The wealth of empires—in Jesus's time and our own—is built off the backs of exploited and impoverished people. But who are the architects of empire? Who are the stabilizers of empire? Who are the gatekeepers of empire? Not the poor. The architects of empire are the senators, the magistrates, and the corporations. The stabilizers and gatekeepers are the storytellers: academics, media, and the church.

The stories we tell about what is moral, what is sin, and what is our responsibility have the capacity to either uphold or upend the imperial order. Far more often than we wish it were true, Christians have upheld empire. We do this more surreptitiously than overtly. We do it as a way of catering to our own fear and anxiety and ego and desire to hoard resources. We do it because it is easier. We do it because transformation is slow, painful, costly work, and we do it because our imaginations are stunted by imperial conditioning. We can imagine writing checks, we can imagine good volunteer projects and mission trips, we can imagine building tiny houses, and we can imagine canned food drives. But can we imagine abolishing poverty? Can we imagine ending homelessness permanently and forever?

Can we imagine a world—or even a single congregation— where drug dealers are as valued and beloved as bishops? Where the sins and spiritual gifts of both are held up to the light and assessed honestly and according to scale?

I think about this tax collector's prayer a lot, especially when I think about Randy, the hand he's been dealt, and how he might try to make sense of it. I think of how he might see himself as a moral failure because we never talk about the immorality of the larger structures of our society or the history we inherit. The individual sins of poor people loom large in our imaginations because the operation of our whole society still hinges on the idea that people are poor through some fault of their own. This, despite the reality that almost half of Americans are poor—and that redistributing the wealth of the tiniest top percentile would be more than enough to end that poverty.

But this tax collector—we choose him for our scapegoat. He has probably lied at some point in his life. He has probably stolen. He has probably done some dirt to other poor people. That is the guilt and the price of his survival. And yet despite the crushing system bearing down on him, he still wants to be a person who does the right thing. He is ashamed he cannot. "Dear God, I am sorry I ripped off that olive farmer and deprived him of money he might have needed to care for his sick daughter. I did it because I also have children. And I will do anything to keep them fed. This is the one chance I had. Be merciful to me, a sinner!"

If Jesus loves that prayer more than the prayer of the Pharisee, it is because Jesus sees the bigger picture. Jesus sees the hard choices the Pharisee has never been forced to make. Jesus sees the life and light in the eyes of the tax collector's children when there is food on the table. Jesus sees the shame and rage on the faces of the peasant farmers being robbed by the empire's extortion, and the shame and rage behind the eyes of the tax collectors who can't secure their survival any other way. Jesus sees the magistrates and senators high above the fray, free to spend their days in deep intellectual debates and comfortable living precisely because the blood of the poor is running in the streets.

And up out of this violence and chaos, one penitent prayer rises to God's ears: the honest reflection of a heart broken by the shame of survival. Jesus hears that prayer. He hears it and he answers: "It's not you, baby. It's the whole damn system that's guilty. Come with me. We'll take it on together."

So, to anyone else out there who is broke, hustling, and blaming themselves: the Bible might not be the thing you think it is. What would it look like to read it with an eye toward poor people?

Exercise: Learn what the Bible says— and doesn't say—about the poor

You might not preach a sermon any time soon. Then again, you might. Either way, it wouldn't hurt to get familiar with the Bible at least enough to know what it does and doesn't say—particularly about stuff like racism, militarism, and poverty for your next hot conversation with Randy.

Read the following texts and then reflect on the questions that follow each.*

Deuteronomy 15:1–2, 7–11

At the end of every seven years you must cancel debts. This is how it is to be done: Every creditor shall cancel any loan they have made to a fellow Israelite. They shall not require payment from anyone among their own people, because the Lord's time for canceling debts has been proclaimed. . . If anyone is poor among your fellow Israelites in any of the towns of the land the Lord your God is giving you, do not be hardhearted or tightfisted toward them. Rather, be openhanded and freely lend them whatever they need. Be careful not to harbor this wicked thought: "The seventh year, the year for canceling debts, is near," so that you do not show ill will toward the needy among your fellow Israelites and give them nothing. They may then appeal to the Lord against you, and you will be found guilty of sin. Give generously to them and do so without a grudging heart; then because of this the Lord your God will bless

---

* If any of this stuff has stoked a fire in your soul, or even just a tiny little ember, you can find more of the same in *We Cry Justice: Reading the Bible with the Poor People's Campaign* (Minneapolis: Broadleaf Books, 2021), edited by Rev. Dr. Liz Theoharis and featuring a number of folks from the Freedom Church of the Poor (including yours truly).

you in all your work and in everything you put your hand to. There will always be poor people in the land. Therefore I command you to be openhanded toward your fellow Israelites who are poor and needy in your land.

1. Have you ever read this text before? If not, what surprised you? If yes, did you notice anything new reading it this time?
2. What do you think Randy would say about this text?

Matthew 19:16–24

Just then a man came up to Jesus and asked, "Teacher, what good thing must I do to get eternal life?"

"Why do you ask me about what is good?" Jesus replied. "There is only One who is good. If you want to enter life, keep the commandments."

"Which ones?" he inquired.

Jesus replied, "'You shall not murder, you shall not commit adultery, you shall not steal, you shall not give false testimony, honor your father and mother,' and 'love your neighbor as yourself.'"

"All these I have kept," the young man said. "What do I still lack?"

Jesus answered, "If you want to be perfect, go, sell your possessions and give to the poor, and you will have treasure in heaven. Then come, follow me."

When the young man heard this, he went away sad, because he had great wealth.

Then Jesus said to his disciples, "Truly I tell you, it is hard for someone who is rich to enter the kingdom of heaven. Again I tell you, it is easier for a camel to go through the eye of a needle than for someone who is rich to enter the kingdom of God."

1. Have you ever read this text before? If not, what surprised you? If yes, did you notice anything new reading it this time?
2. What do you think Randy would say about this text?

James 5:1–6

Now listen, you rich people, weep and wail because of the misery that is coming on you. Your wealth has rotted, and moths have eaten your clothes. Your gold and silver are corroded. Their corrosion will testify against you and eat your flesh like fire. You have hoarded wealth in the last days. Look! The wages you failed to pay the workers who mowed your fields are crying out against you. The cries of the harvesters have reached the ears of the Lord Almighty. You have lived on earth in luxury and self-indulgence. You have fattened yourselves in the day of slaughter. You have condemned and murdered the innocent one, who was not opposing you.

1. Have you ever read this text before? If not, what surprised you? If yes, did you notice anything new reading it this time?
2. What do you think Randy would say about this text?

7

Rule Seven: Rehome Randy

So let's say that you and Randy have been talking for a while now. Maybe he has opened up to you a bit. Maybe you have a better idea of where he's coming from and why he shacked up with The First Church of White Christian Nationalism. Even though you can't stand them, you can see he's getting a legitimate need met there: community, recovery support, free childcare, belonging, purpose, a sense of being connected to something bigger than himself, you name it.

Or maybe your Randy isn't the churchgoing type. Maybe he watches preachers on cable TV and it strikes a chord. Or maybe he logs into Truth Social and far-right chat groups, and all that content creates this entire universe for him of conspiracy theory and distorted Christianity and anti-Black racism and xenophobia.

Either way, whichever corner of Randyland he's coming from, he recognizes at this juncture that you've bothered to come out to visit him there a couple times. Maybe Randy has even heard you out a few times as you've talked about racial justice or why discrimination against LGBTQ people is wrong. Maybe something in him seems movable where there was previously a brick wall.

So now what?

Friends: this is a critical juncture in counter-recruitment. Frankly, it's also the place where we presently seem to lose the most people. Why? Because if and when Randy decides he just can't rock with the First Church of White Christian Nationalism in good conscience any longer, he needs to find a new social, political, spiritual, and communal home. And right now, alternative options that would honestly make any sense to Randy are pretty hard to come by.

"Oh dang," you're saying (I can hear you). Yes, dang is right. Where are you going to send him? Aunt Barb already threw him out twice.

Here's where this book really starts to demand more of your commitment, your strategic thinking, and your willingness to counter White Christian nationalism for the long haul. If counter-recruitment were simply a matter of Randy Plug-and-Play, in which you unhook Randy from the old system and hook him up to a new one, this would all be a lot simpler. And we as a nation probably wouldn't be neck-deep in insurrectionist horse-shit at this late hour.

Alas. So here I am, asking you to help actually build the new system into which we will plug Randy. That's right. If all goes well, you won't just be a Randy Whisperer by the end of this book. You'll also be an architect of social support systems, an organizer of community institutions, and a popular educator.

In short: you'll be a movement builder.

Where is Randy supposed to go?

"Okay, fine, but I don't want to bother with all that," you might be saying. "I'm just here to get Randy off the Trump Train!" Sure, I hear you. But it isn't simply detached intellectual ideas that got him on that train in the first place, so it's not just gonna be intellectual debates that get him off it.

Here, again, is the uneven playing field we're on, wherein the architects of White Christian nationalism are frolicking in the greenest, grassiest part of the field while you and I are tripping over broken glass and rusty nails and twisting our ankles on the other side (is our side even a field? It looks more like an arsenic mine).

For a solid few generations now, the push to privatize our entire society—a dastardly bipartisan affair called "neoliberalism"—has left most of our infrastructure pretty gutted. Stuff that was once considered apolitically important for the public good (housing! the social safety net! public schools! meaningful and accessible health care!) has now not only been vastly defunded but also frequently vilified by White Christian nationalism and by no shortage of neoliberals. And in this country, we know that *vilified* just about always means *racialized* (see the "welfare queen" trope hawked by Nixon and Reagan, which drove Clinton to slash that entire system to bits).

At the same time—and the two things are not unrelated— the economy has gotten worse and worse. It's possible Randy's dad and granddad did their fair share of pissing and moaning about big government. But statistically, they're far more likely than Randy to have benefited from union jobs, Social Security, and Medicare. Randy comes along, perhaps a child of the 1980s or 1990s, and, as would be his fate in many little towns all over this country, is born into economic and social freefall. Not only are wages and unionization down; union halls, mainline churches, the Elks Club, the bingo hall, and a number of social networks accessible to regular-ass people are also on the decline. So, all these structural changes haven't just tanked the economic livelihoods of millions of Americans; they've also shuttered countless community institutions, leaving lots of folks more lonely and isolated than ever.

But not at the First Church of White Christian Nationalism! They're growing and growing every day. And the bigger they get, the more they invest in youth programs and community outreach.

So, if Randy's gonna leave the First Church of WCN, as we hope he will, here is the main question: Where will he go to find a sense of belonging? Where will he find an alternative community, structure, and yes, even institution to look out for him?

While there are hundreds of thousands of congregations across the country, many of which do not lean in the direction of White Christian nationalism, the vast majority of these are small and getting smaller—in terms of budget, in terms of people, in terms of impact, and in terms of vision. The COVID-19 pandemic only accelerated this shrinking. There are, of course, feisty little (and even a few large) churches in this vein that are absolutely alive and on fire for the holy work of justice. But they are spread thin, far, and wide. And the odds of Randy being able to find one of those churches in his neck of the woods? Not great.

And yet, this is exactly what he needs: not church just for the sake of going to church but a community institution that concerns itself with Randy's life in a holistic way. A group of people who regularly gather in a physical place, around the work of meeting both material needs and also caring for a person's soul. Not in the predatory, exploitative, oppressive way that the First Church of WCN does; in a way that actually boosts the liberation of all people.

YOU: Are you telling me to plant a goddamn CHURCH?!

ME: I did not use those exact words.

Listen. I don't care if you plant a religious community, or a garden, or a robust and somewhat politicized lemonade stand.

What I do care about is that we find a way to bring the countless Randys and Brandys and Andys of this country into the fold in an effective, long-lasting, and transformative way. We need them woven into deep relationships with lots of other people, across many lines of difference, with a shared commitment to the daily work of justice and collective survival for all people—all races, all genders, all sexual orientations, all abilities, all religions.

Presently, we simply do not have the network of community-based institutions we need to achieve that goal. Door-knocking and campaigns and all that are fine. But we aren't going to door-knock and campaign our way out of this toxic, death-dealing morass. There is no shortcut here. People first need to have their immediate survival needs taken seriously in some way, and they simultaneously need to have a meaningful community of relationships. And then on top of that (also simultaneously), they need to be plugged into long-term education and leadership development. This is the foundation upon which you can then layer all the door-knocking your heart desires.

Coincidentally, houses of worship are structured just this way. Walk through the week with a little, predominantly White Baptist church out in the Kansas sticks, or with a large and historic Black congregation in the heart of Washington DC. In both places, you will find people regularly sharing meals, reading books together, checking in on their most vulnerable members, and studying up on how to live out their deepest values in community in the middle of this hurting world. This is why some faith communities have been on the front lines of resisting authoritarian movements throughout history. Others, of course, have propped up those very same movements. Religion, like any powerful thing, can either be wielded as a weapon of oppression or a tool of liberation.

The Redneck Freedom Church of the Poor

Imagine if justice-loving Christians had a network of liberation-oriented communities of faith—a constellation of churches and other spiritual homes—that could capture and care for Randy just as readily as the First Church of White Christian Nationalism did. We could call this network the Freedom Church of the Poor, a phrase first coined by Dr. King in the last year of his life to describe the building of a "nonviolent army of the poor" as a leading and transformative social force for justice and mercy. In this Freedom Church network, Randy would discover people just like him, working every day to take care of one another and learn more about themselves and the world around them, alongside a whole bunch of other people who he may have once believed he had nothing in common with.

In the Freedom Church of the Poor, nobody's going to make you sing happy-clappy songs for Jesus on Sunday morning. But we are going to recruit you to join us in planting thousands of little nodes of the network, strung together from Decatur to San Antonio. No two will be exactly alike. But we need them to be unified enough on the things that matter and effective enough to catch a lot of regular-ass people.

In the Freedom Church of the Poor, your cousin Randy is building real-world relationships, mutual accountability, mutual care, knowledge, a common culture, strategic alliances, and power with other poor people from every race and creed and corner of this country. And he's even building those connections with a few folks who aren't poor themselves but who are committed enough to the values of liberty and justice for all that they're willing to throw everything they've got behind Freedom Church: scholars, faith leaders, organizers, artists, people of conscience and good-will from every background you can think of.

Maybe for you, being part of any faith-based network feels like a bridge too far. I get that. Looking around at the state of religion in this country probably gives you plenty of reasons to want to run far, far away. But the thing is, in the Freedom Church of the Poor, nobody's going to convert you to anything except the liberation of all people, starting from the bottom.

Can you imagine it? Randy! Throwing down for Black and Brown people. Throwing down for LGBTQ people. Throwing down for reproductive justice. Throwing down for Indigenous sovereignty. Throwing down for an end to wars of US aggression. Throwing down for every single person's right to housing, health care, and quality education from birth to death, including his own. Randy. Your cousin Randy!

YOU: Actually, no. I can't imagine it. This is all still sounding like pie in the sky.

ME: You need more real-life Randy stories to illustrate this possibility?

YOU: You have them?

ME: Silver and gold have I none, but such as I have, give I thee. In Randy stories.

Let's take a trip to rural Washington State

When my co-pastor Cedar Monroe and I were just getting started at Chaplains on the Harbor, we spent most of our time grocery shopping. Our base was hungry people, so there was never any point in trying to hold a meeting without food. We grew beyond the groceries, of course; eventually we planted a wide network of survival support, political education, and leadership development for poor, homeless, and incarcerated Randys, Brandys, and Andys.

But what did this look like day to day? Slow and soggy, mostly. Rural life moves at a rural pace; also, it rains a lot out here. But we built a steady routine and used consistency to help us grow our numbers. On Sundays, we borrowed space at a downtown church to host a free community dinner, always with good, hot, abundant food. While most of the same folks wouldn't darken the door of that same church on Sunday morning to save their lives, they were incredibly regular at Sunday dinner.

And not just for the meal. People were hungry for community. They were hungry for a place to get out of the rain and charge their phones. They were hungry for a place where they knew someone would be checking on them to make sure they were okay. And on the Sundays when they were definitely not okay, folks knew they could still show up and be seen, heard, respected, and treated like whole-ass human beings instead of corrupt criminals or sad charity cases.

It sounds basic, but there's actually a whole lot of labor, time, skill, and creative thinking that goes into making a space like this possible for poor people. Sunday dinner became established as a trusted street institution for folks who were unhoused, squatting, or tenants in the supremely overpriced and run-down apartments around the church. A lot of folks were also dealing with legal issues, bouncing in and out of jail, and often (though not always) involved in the drug economy. Why? Because it's an economy. It's a job. When there aren't other jobs available—because of where you live, or what pops up on your background check—people will do what they need to do to survive and feed their kids.

Anyway, what all this meant for Sunday dinner was that we were constantly navigating crises, and we had to keep organizing in the thick of it. We organized the feeding, community building, and peacekeeping while maintaining our space as a "sanctuary" from law enforcement. This generally meant that cops did not have permission to enter our space, a long-standing claim permitted to houses of worship. If they wanted to question people or take people in, they had to wait on the doorstep, at the property line, or across the street. At the church entrance, we placed a door mat that read: "Come Back with a Warrant."

During Sunday dinner, we welcomed folks in and organized political education sessions, truth commissions, strategy sessions on how to contend with encampment sweeps and evictions, national movement-building tours, and arts and culture events. All this happened in the same space and at the same time as Sunday dinner, while holding down Sunday dinner. Why? Because without the anchor of Sunday dinner, all the other competing crises in folks' daily lives would overshadow the organizing.

It's not realistic to ask a human being to choose between a meeting or hustling up a few dollars for their next meal. When you force people into this choice, you force poor people out of the meeting. Just feed folks for free at the goddamn meeting. And hold the meeting in a space where people don't have to worry about the police lying in wait to pick them up on their petty theft charge from Walmart. And make all your meeting content accessible for people with a wide range of literacy ability. And be ready to provide some basic first aid as needed.

Anyway, that was just Sunday! Every other day of the week, we fed people, did street outreach, made jail and hospital and encampment visits, published a jail and prison newsletter with statewide circulation, ran a small farm, and, during the cold weather, hosted a shelter.

Whew, I'm wore out and stressed out just typing that list. Nobody said igniting the revolution in Randyland was gonna be light work!

What progressive organizing gets wrong

It is this experience that has given me a very clear response to the question "What is wrong with liberal/progressive/left organizing in the United States of America?"

Well, for starters, the food is bad and there's not enough of it. Compare the food at your bike lane ballot initiative meeting to a Baptist potluck. Now ask yourself honestly (Jesus is watching) where you'd rather be if you were a hungry person. I know I don't need to elaborate here; just pass me the deviled eggs and pound cake.

Second, liberals and progressives do not have an adequate religious strategy. A mass movement for transformation in our society is absolutely going to require a broad multifaith coalition, and that has been true for every effective social movement in our history. Since this book is focused on the Randy contingent of that coalition, I'm talking about the strategic involvement of Christians, and especially Protestants. Despite the great disaffiliation of so many folks, the United States right now is still about 64 percent Christian. And there are somewhere around 140 million Protestants in the United States—that's about 43 percent of the entire country.

Now, a caveat: it is true that a lot of Randys are not Protestant. Plenty are Catholic, plenty claim no religion, and a small but growing number adhere to earth-based spirituality. The changing religious demographics of Randyland are real, and they merit their own book. For the sake of brevity, I'm going with here-and-now numbers. Currently, Protestantism is still in first place for Randys who are Gen X and older—although nobody knows for how long. Millennial Randys are their own spiritual breed; in my corner of the earth, a whole bunch of them are MAGA heathens (by "heathen" I mean literal Norse pagans), but just as many are deeply apolitical and irreligious. Check the endnotes for a helpful tool on what the religious landscape might be in your corner of the country.

Still, more Protestants live in the US than any other nation on earth. So, if you're trying to build a mass movement for justice and the common good, that's a hell of a lot of people to ignore.

The third problem with liberal and progressive organizing in the US is that poor people aren't treated as central to it, relationally or strategically. A lot of things factor into this. As union membership has dropped sharply over the last century, many poor and working-class people have lost their access and their relationship to progressive organizing spaces. With the majority of struggling Americans now absent, organizing spaces have become increasingly academic and professionalized. Additionally, a lot of electoral organizing is attached to the Democratic Party. Poor people vote far less often than people in other class demographics, mainly because of transportation issues, illness and disability, difficulty taking off work, and plain old voter intimidation and suppression. Because poor people don't vote, their zip codes aren't highly prioritized in many liberal and progressive voter turnout efforts.

This isn't because all the liberals and progressives in America got together one day and decided that electoral work was more important than everything else, and screw all the nonvoters. The entire funding infrastructure of the liberal and progressive movement is pretty singularly focused on elections, to the point that every four years, any group getting notable foundation funding basically has to shelve all their other work (education, community building, whatever) and reorient to electoral work.

Don't get me wrong: elections matter. In fact, they matter too much for us to keep ignoring poor people, who make up one of the largest untapped voting blocs in the country. Today, national elections that determine the futures of hundreds of millions of people hinge on a few suburbs and exurbs in a few battleground ·

states. But imagine the power that could be unleashed if poor people were brought into the voting process and kept there as fully empowered agents of political change. We wouldn't have to keep hearing about the ten White ladies in White Lady Suburb #45 who we need to win over. Hell, we might even end up with thousands of Randy-filled pickup trucks on our side.

In case you hadn't noticed, White Christian nationalists have started to figure this out. Critically, they understand that their aspirations in the electoral arena require them to organize in other arenas as well. In addition to GOTV efforts, they've built churches, they've built schools, they've built disaster relief organizations, they've built publishing houses, they've built media infrastructure, they've built entertainment and cultural institutions, they've built militias . . . I could go on. I'm not saying we need to imitate White Christian nationalism's strategy lock, stock, and barrel. But it is worth noting: liberals and progressives, you've put all your eggs in the elections basket, with almost none of the institutional, community-based infrastructure to hold it together, and you're still losing more often than you're winning. Maybe it's time to try some new things.

Does Randy even vote?

But why don't poor people vote? Here's what microeconomist Robert Paul Hartley writes in a report on the power of poor and low-income Americans for the Poor People's Campaign:

> Relative to the rest of the population, lower-income Americans are more likely than those at higher incomes to not vote because of issues like transportation problems or illness/disability, and less likely relative to higher

income Americans to not vote because of time conflicts, general busyness, or travel. These descriptive comparisons suggest that lower- and higher-income Americans are similar in nonvoting patterns related to how candidates connect to their issues or belief that their vote matters. However, the electorate differs by income status in that low-income nonvoters are more constrained by issues out of their control (transportation, illness/disability) compared to higher-income nonvoters that report being busy or away.

Organizers, progressives, people of faith, and people of plain damn moral conscience who want to see a fairer country simply cannot afford to keep ignoring Randyland and all the other broke-ass zip codes across America. More people are falling into poverty every single day. That means more people are falling into the kinds of crises with which professionalized, jargony, and stingy-with-the-food methods of organizing cannot compete. These kinds of crises get in the way of doing democracy.

If you want a mass base of folks ready to fight for their own literal survival and strengthen the survival odds of everyone else, you have got to invest in poor folks as political actors, thinkers, and leaders. Ignore Randy and the rest of us and see where it gets you.

In fact, we're the ones who have the power to turn this thing around in many, many ways—including at the ballot box. Economist Hartley here again:

It is well documented that low-income voters are not as likely to show up at the polls. However, this is a relatively large potential voting population with similar voting trends and mobilization possibilities as the rest of the population. After the 2016 presidential election, both those with low income and those with relatively higher income increased turnout by nearly the same percentage-point change for the 2018 midterm elections. Not only is the potential low-income voting population relatively large compared to the total electorate by state, there are several important election states in which low income voting at the rates of the rest of the population would match or exceed recent election margins of victory.

In other words, even if electoral organizing is all you care about, poor people have got the numbers you want. Stop ignoring us. Stop thinking about us as secondary to the goal of social transformation. You won't move this country without me and Randy and all our other cousins.

False prophets in Randyland

Coincidentally, just as there are roughly 140 million Protestants in America, there also happen to be 140 million poor people in the United States. This makes us both the wealthiest nation in the history of the planet and the nation with the highest rate of poverty in the so-called "developed" world.*

As easy as it is to focus on the violent, loudmouth, anti–poor people rhetoric of White Christian nationalists, we must also note this: both liberals and conservatives at the top of the

---

* Put another way: the most Protestant nation in the world has the worst inequality in the world. Weird. It's almost like there might be a correlation here.

economic food chain are united in their common cause to defend their wealth. This is also true of both evangelicals and mainline Christians.

For those of you who don't know much about the different flavors of Christianity, it's important to understand just how wealthy many liberal mainline Christians are. Despite espousing a different sort of God-talk than evangelicals or Pentecostals, mainliners are often more out of touch with poor people than any other thread of Christianity.

Episcopalians, as the bougiest stop on the mainline, have the highest family income of any Christian denomination in the nation. Meanwhile, the Assemblies of God, American Baptists, Church of God In Christ, National Baptists, and Jehovah's Witnesses—most of which trend more conservative and are far more likely to be Randy's go-to neighborhood church—have the lowest household incomes among all US religious groups. The denominational class divide in many ways compounds political division. When I'm walking down the street in a poor neighborhood in Anytown USA, I feel very confident that I will stumble across six shady bars, a cop shop, a VFW hall, and at least four different highly conservative Christian denominations. I feel much less confident that I would encounter even one Episcopal or Presbyterian Church, let alone the headquarters of a progressive nonprofit.

All these more conservative denominations will duke it out over baptism, why Jesus died on the cross, how long the Holy Spirit thinks your skirt should be, and what the staples of a church potluck are. And yet somehow, even when their own pews are full of broke-ass folks like me and Randy, they haven't managed to drown out White Christian nationalism's fundamental heresies.

So how did a religion centered on the worship of Jesus—a refugee born in a barn who lived and died preaching, teaching, and practicing that the last shall be first and the first shall be last—morph into America's White Christian nationalism? There could be a whole book on that question, and this is not that book. So, here's a short answer: imperialism and capitalism, for starters. There's also been a healthy dose of anti-liberation sentiment baked into the Protestant pie from day one. Martin Luther's own 1525 advice to the German princes on how to handle peasant uprisings summarizes it real blunt: "Stab, smite, slay, whoever can!"

Certainly, this anti-poor-people, imperial theology has not been without challengers (hat tip to everyone from Thomas Müntzer to Harriet Tubman!). But to really contend with White Christian nationalism, we have to go deep into its theological roots. Why? Because the theological architects of this movement are surely doing their homework and have built themselves quite a fortress. We're gonna have to do our fair share of work and study to find and widen the cracks in their foundations—while at the same time laying our own.

So what is the cornerstone of the Freedom Church of the Poor? How is this different from the cornerstone of the First Church of White Christian Nationalism?

Simple. The poor are the cornerstone of the Freedom Church of the Poor. We, the 140 million poor people in America, as the scripture says, are the stone that the builders of this society have rejected for over four hundred years. In the Freedom Church of the Poor, we are the cornerstone. And through the labor of the Freedom Church of the Poor, we become the cornerstone of this entire society.

The First Church of White Christian Nationalism might give you a lot of mushy, feel-good talk about how much they loooooove the poor—how they cut fat checks to the local soup kitchen, how they volunteer there every month, how they even have several people at the church who were once homeless themselves but ever since they found Jesus have been able to bootstrap their way out of poverty and sin and make their way back to that ultimate American idol: respectability.

This is not love.

So, what is?

To love Randy

To love the poor means to ask: Why are so many of us poor in the first place? It means not settling for magical thinking in lieu of real answers to this question.

To love the poor means despising the system that creates poverty in the first place and actively working to dismantle it.

To love the poor means looking beyond the good works or sins of individual poor people to the manufactured situation of an entire class: the poor. The poor were the class to which Jesus himself belonged, the class into which he was born, raised, crucified, the class to which he first appeared upon his resurrection.

To love the poor means to fight for poor people's lives and dignity. Charity does not accomplish this. Advocating for the poor without listening to the poor does not accomplish this. Poor people are neither voiceless nor powerless: we are systematically silenced and disenfranchised.

One uncomfortable thing that White Christian nationalism and US liberalism have in common is this: both are guilty, in their own ways, of using the poor. They both utilize the poor for their own aims—alternately as scapegoats and poster children, frequently as rhetorical and political footballs, and always as shields to fend off valid critique.

Both claim to love the good kind of poor people: the deserving kind, according to each camp's respective and arbitrary definitions. White Christian nationalism is often candid about which kind of poor people are the wrong kind (the gay ones, the ones who want access to abortions, the ones who struggle with addiction, the intensely racialized so-called "welfare queens," and so on). Progressives tend to have a shorter list of the "wrong" kind of poor people.

But your cousin Randy is definitely on it.

To love the poor means to love Randy. To defend Randy's human rights and to see his place in a broader movement for the thriving of all people. Even when he's fucking up and dancing on your last nerve.

Exercise: If you build it, Randy will come

Sit with the following questions and see if you can come up with answers that start to give shape to the kind of community that would genuinely interest Randy and pull him into a movement for justice and dignity for all people.

1. Think about the most compelling, immediate offering that gets Randy through the front door. Is it having a regular place to do laundry? Hot lunch? Free Wi-Fi and coffee? List any and all **material aid** that you think would get his attention.

2. Once Randy's in there, what kind of environment would it take to get him comfortable engaging with other people from all walks of life and different backgrounds? Would keeping music or movies on in the background loosen him up? What about a free library? Would an open mic night be interesting to him, or would it freak him out? Think along the lines of **arts and culture** and list what you think would hook him.

3. So Randy's in there and he's beyond the mingling stage—he's a regular and he's making some good connections and building relationships. How do you engage him in **political education**? Do you start with movies? Do you hold a weekly time to read through the local paper as a group and see what issues grab him most? What kind of guest speakers might interest him?

4. How do you shift engaged Randy to the next level and get him leading, facilitating, and sharing his expertise and experience? What kind of support or encouragement might Randy need in order to **develop as a leader**? For some folks, if they're really shy, it might be most comfortable to start really small and behind the scenes, setting up chairs beforehand or washing dishes after a group. But after a few rounds of that, you nudge them forward and encourage them to take on a more visible role. What are some of Randy's strengths, as well as some areas he's less confident? (Hint: if you don't know, ASK RANDY!)

8

Rule Eight: Stop Blaming People and Start Organizing Them

Let me tell you some stories from the frontlines of this Freedom Church of the Poor movement that is already being built to effectively counter White Christian nationalism across this country. It's small and scrappy but very much alive. It's kind of like a sudden rash of spring buds popping up in the wasteland of America's political terrain.

Story #1: Our pastor regularly visited folks in the county jail—not to proselytize but simply to be present with them and find out what they were dealing with. The day that Donald Trump won the 2016 presidential election was a jail visit day, and our pastor reported that the young rednecks in jail were scared and flipping out. "I can't believe this," one nineteen-year-old guy behind bars said to the pastor about Trump's election. "This is really, really bad!"

You wouldn't know this, though, if you read the Associated Press coverage of our county that came out shortly after the election. That's because a journalist with the AP called up our pastor, got permission to come visit our feeding program, and immediately cherrypicked the most bigoted, lonely, half-cocked older folks they could find expressly for the purpose of getting them to talk about how excited they were about Trump's victory. Never mind that they were not at all representative of the significant swaths of young, poor, disenfranchised people in town, many of whom couldn't vote because they were locked up or had outstanding warrants and who disliked Trump as much if not more than your local liberal Lutheran pastor.

That's the power of building a Freedom Church of the Poor, or Freedom Shul of the Poor, or Freedom Lemonade Stand of the Poor: you get to see what's actually happening on the ground in poor communities that are getting scapegoated for all of society's ills. And you get to understand that there are far more people there to work with than any newspaper will ever admit.

Story #2: Our redneck Freedom Church of the Poor team got a little bit of grant money, so we decided to do a study trip to Mississippi. There we met with Black organizers, faith leaders, and Civil Rights veterans, to learn from their work (I described the trip in greater detail in the introduction). In preparation for the trip, my coworker Candy—the former biker and street fighter, now in recovery and running our shelter—took it upon herself to independently research Emmett Till's case, which she had never learned about before.

Candy was so galled, sickened, and outraged by what she learned that she wrote an entire series on the Till case for our jail and prison newsletter, *The Holy Hustler*. She wrote it all out by hand because she couldn't type. That series circulated through every prison in the state, particularly through the White prison gangs that made up much of the incarcerated membership of our Freedom Church.

Story #3: A grizzled, harsh, old drug dealer, one of our most faithful Sunday dinner guests, had long nursed a grudge against the right-wing religious shelter provider in town for throwing him out of their program. He was not someone who would have called himself anyone's ally, for any reason. But living on the edge of survival tends to force you into alliances with other folks out there as well.

One day, he found out that this same shelter provider was refusing to host LGBTQ homeless people. "Well," he growled, "I guess I have to be okay with gay people now—because they're screwing them over too."

Story #4: At our local city council meetings, it was standard for the city code enforcement officer to sit right next to the mayor—especially anytime there were public conversations about "illegal camping" (i.e., trying to survive without housing). Why? Because Code Enforcement was the department tasked with evicting people from their campsites and bulldozing the makeshift shelters they'd built for themselves. I guess Code Enforcement and the mayor leaned on each other for moral support in those meetings because it hurt their feelings to be called "inhumane" by the people whose homes they were demolishing.

Anyway, that seating arrangement, along with a lot of vitriol and threats from other meeting attendees, made for a pretty hostile environment. So, lots of the time, folks who were unhoused didn't feel safe coming to the meetings in person. As a workaround, our lead pastor at the redneck Freedom Church of the Poor and I would film the city council meetings on our phones.

We would then take that footage to the right-wing Christian shelter mentioned in Story #3 above, because it was the main spot in town for free lunch. That way, folks living on the streets or in the shelter could catch up on what had happened at the city council meeting. Eventually, we got permanently banned from that shelter for this kind of organizing. (But not before we bummed free lunch and made the democratic process more accessible for poor people.)

Story #5: Through our Poor People's Campaign network, two of the women on our team (think: Randy's mom and sister; we'll call them Candy and her daughter Sandy) got invited to spend a week at an organizers training in North Carolina. Led by fast food employees in the Union of Southern Service Workers, the training mixed political education on the economy with concrete workplace organizing skills.

So these two got dropped in middle-of-nowhere rural North Carolina, met up with a Black-led coalition of workers from Wendy's and McDonald's, and started pounding the fast food pavement to help organize a massive strike. And they effing loved every minute of it. They came back to our podunk White-trash county totally on fire and ready to organize harder. And we heard stories from organizers across the country of how strong and passionate Candy's and Sandy's leadership was, how proudly and powerfully they represented their work to organize homeless folks back home, and how much they had to teach other poor people from across the country.

Story #6: My friend and coworker, a formerly homeless veteran in recovery from addiction who I'll call Xandy, traveled to Washington DC with the Poor People's Campaign. When Xandy came to DC, he sat on a panel hosted by Senator Elizabeth Warren's office alongside several remarkable people. Xandy testified alongside Kenia Alcocer, an undocumented Latinx mother, with her young daughter in her arms, testifying about living in daily fear of family separation. And alongside Vanessa Nosie, an Apache mother demanding that the desecration of her people's holiest mountain via mining be halted. And alongside several other poor people, from West Virginia to Flint, Michigan.

He also testified alongside Pamela Rush, a Black mother from Lowndes County, Alabama, who, along with her children, was forced to sleep with a CPAP machine because of the poisonous levels of mold and exposed raw sewage in the mobile home in which she lived. She had paid more than four times the value of that trailer in high interest fees.

A heartbreaking side note to that day: Rush would die in July 2020 after contracting COVID. But in the words of two of her friends, journalist and author Catherine Coleman Flowers and William J. Barber III:

> Before the coronavirus, Pam was dealing with the pandemic of poverty, living as one of the nation's 140 million poor people—not through any fault of her own, but as a victim of vicious systems of predatory lending, economic exploitation, and disinvestment. Before the coronavirus, Pam was living as a Black woman in America, which put her at a 21% higher risk of exposure to long-term air pollution, directly increasing her risk of morbidity from the virus. Before the coronavirus, Pam lived in rural Alabama—one of the 13 states that have resisted implementing Medicaid expansion—as one of

the nation's 27.5 million uninsured people. She lived as one of the thousands of people in our nation who lack access to proper plumbing, with no federal guarantee of clean water or sanitation services so urgently needed to survive this pandemic. Before the coronavirus, Pam also lived in a state that sought to limit her ability to petition the government for a redress of grievances through rampant modern voter suppression tactics. This virus, like a heat-seeking missile, zeroed in on Pam. The intersections of poverty, environmental injustice, climate change, and racial and health disparities placed multiple targets on her back. How do we remember her? We will tell her story. And we will fight for policies that will prevent others in the same situation as Pamela Sue Rush to give up their lives too soon. For her children, we will ensure that her legacy lives on.

Xandy delivered his testimony on surviving as a homeless millennial veteran in a county with almost no support for addicts to speak of. Bishop William J. Barber II introduced all the panelists as the moral and spiritual authorities America most needs to hear. And for an hour, some of the most powerful people in the country had to listen, whether they wanted to or not.

These are just a few of the stories I've had the honor to witness and participate in firsthand, but there are so many more.

SURJ (Showing Up for Racial Justice) has played a critical role in shifting the political terrain in poor, majority-White communities across the South and Appalachia, winning key state and local campaigns against White Christian nationalist candidates by bringing poor Whites into multiracial, pro-democracy organizing.

Christians Against Christian Nationalism, a campaign anchored by the Baptist Joint Committee, has mounted a nationwide effort to disrupt the distorted moral narrative of White Christian nationalism and educate a vast political swath of Christians on its dangers.

Faithful America has faithfully shown up to counter Mike Flynn's "Reawaken America" circus sideshow with all kinds of creative, love-and-justice-focused messaging.

And Rev. Caleb Campbell, after losing 80 percent of his Evangelical congregation in Arizona to White Christian nationalist churches in the wake of the 2016 election, dubbed those lost sheep his "mission field." He has written a book and launched a campaign to help people bring them back—not by appeasing any fascist tendencies or talk but by doubling down on the Bible's commandments toward love, impartiality, truth, mercy, and justice.

Lessons learned

What has all this taught me? That building this movement is not only possible in the reddest of red counties on the American electoral map, but that it's necessary. And also that, sometimes, it's a lot of goddamn fun.

The way we planted our outpost of the Freedom Church of the Poor in rural Washington—sheltered by the church, nurturing a politics of liberation, and answerable first and foremost to the poor of Randyland—allowed us to try a bunch of stuff that most churches and most progressive organizations rarely do. In order to shift the framework from blaming people to organizing them, you have to be present on the ground in some instrumental ways.

So, what has this model of organizing allowed us to do?

First, it allowed us to organize a multiracial coalition led by the poorest people in the county: people who are homeless, incarcerated, on public assistance, disabled, involved in the drug trade or survival sex work—and the church ladies who have their backs.

Second, it helped us to unify poor and working people (including Randy, even when he's making some really shitty political and personal choices) across lines of racial and religious division to build power in countering White Christian nationalist policy violence and social violence.

Third, it made it possible for us to sue the municipality twice in federal court—in defense of homeless people's human, constitutional, and treaty rights. Oh, and it made it possible to build a congregation of 600 poor people, testify before Congress and the Senate, and buy a farm.

So how did we do this?

Well, for two years, we did nothing but build trust (a.k.a. shut up and feed people).

We treated people like leaders—because they already are, a fact we'll learn if we pay enough attention.

We organized around meeting immediate material, social, and spiritual needs, coupled with a commitment to political education, leadership development, and power-building (funerals, food programs, harm reduction, and jail support, among other things).

We leaned on the institutional church for legal services, security muscle, funding, and infrastructure support.

And we had an explicit and inclusive moral, faith-based narrative: God wants everybody in and nobody out in the project of survival and dignity.

It's important to note that we did all of this with the critical support of a religious denomination. To faith folks and non-faith folks alike: for all the baggage that religion (especially Christianity) in America carries, there are unique, strategic opportunities available when you leverage a faith community as your model, vehicle, and container for organizing to counter White Christian nationalism.

Leveraging the muscle of the church for revolutionary change

Organizing through the church should come with a how-to guide of its own.

First, the opportunities. Faith communities are already on the ground: pre-organized, oriented to meeting both immediate needs and holding out a person-centered, long-arc-of-the-universe worldview. This means they present a huge opportunity for movement-building in the hardest-hit places. White Christian nationalism has taken full advantage of churches. Why can't we?

Faith communities can leverage land, buildings, legal muscle, administrative infrastructure, a volunteer base, a moral and theological framework, strategic visibility, ritual, fundraising networks, and more. Partnering with a bishop allowed us to go toe-to-toe with entrenched political powers (including a sharky city attorney whom no local consul dared cross). Working with a church meant we always had "outside eyes" on our local situations when things got hot. I'm pretty sure if we hadn't had those partnerships, we would have faced a lot more violent retaliation than we did.

But let me back for a minute and be extremely clear: our little Freedom Church of the Poor in Randyland did not come up with these ideas on our own. While both my cofounder and I are Randyland born-and-raised, we both also had the chance to break out of those bubbles, specifically to study liberation theology.

I had left church by the time I was fifteen for reasons previously stated (the anti-LGBTQ stuff). Then, when I was twenty—and not looking for churchy shit at all but rather just trying to live my best young wild revolutionary life and learn about socialism—I got a scholarship to study liberation theology on the ground in El Salvador.

I spent a month living there with nuns, other students, and Christian base communities: rural, poor, peasant communities that had come together in the lead-up to El Salvador's civil war. I found myself sitting in Bible studies with people who were using the text to simultaneously teach themselves how to read and how to critique capitalism's abuses of the poor.

One morning, I walked into a Sunday school confirmation class full of fourteen-year-old farm kids analyzing the Central American Free Trade Agreement under the instruction of one of the nuns, who said something to the effect of "Jesus wants us to have abundant life, and this policy robs us of our lives and livelihood, so it is our Christian responsibility to resist it." I met community after community of rural poor church people who, in so many ways, had common cause with the rural poor church community I came up in. But the base communities I met with in El Salvador practiced and preached an entirely different theology, and this pointed them toward an entirely different political and economic orientation. And the church stood with them through it all: through the war, through countless massacres and cover-ups, through the ongoing economic violence of neoliberalism.

The people I met were clear that every time they suffered at the hands of imperialist abuse, Christ suffered with them. And every time they organized to assert their dignity and defend their lives, Christ rose with them and in them.

This experience grabbed me so hard that I came back home and said, "I need to learn how to do this in the US, and I need to meet whoever else is doing it." At that time, Dr. James Cone, the famed author of *A Black Theology of Liberation* and *The Cross and the Lynching Tree*, was still alive and still teaching at Union Theological Seminary, so I enrolled there. I met Rev. Dr. Liz Theoharis on my first day of orientation in 2007, as she was leading a Bible study. The rest is history. I've been leveraging the institutional church in defense of the poor of Randyland ever since.

Of course, it's not always smooth sailing. There are plenty of challenges that come with organizing through faith communities too. Just like everywhere else, there can be a real fear of backlash. Some church people frankly have a fear of the poor, especially when you start talking about the leadership of the poor. But there's also simply a fear of proximity to pain and crisis. Many churches have functioned as nice, stable social clubs for a long time, and that can be a tough bubble to crack.

Most denominations are not structured to accommodate movement work: not administratively, not financially, not legally. If you want them to take it on, or if you want to at least borrow some of their structures or resources and put them to use for this cause, you will often have to push them every inch of the way.

Church people need at least as much (if not more) organizing training and political education as any Randy off the street. Basically, church institutions have been the maintainers of hegemony and have a lot of deprogramming to do. I can't speak to how this may or may not cut across religious traditions other than Christianity. But it's probably wise to keep in mind, with any institution, that change can be an agonizingly slow process and that you're always gonna be stretched between the trade-off of pace versus power. We were tempted weekly (often daily!) to throw in the towel on partnering with an institution because of how damn slow they go. Still, we wouldn't have been able to accomplish even half of what we did without them.

What are some of the challenges of this model, beyond just working with faith communities? I can't lie: money's tight, and sometimes people might try to shoot you.

But I'm convinced that the opportunities outweigh the challenges just about every day. Because here's the dirty little secret that might scare some liberals and progressives but sure as hell scares White Christian nationalists even more:

This shit is replicable.
This shit is scalable.
This shit is wildly popular in Randyland.

Exercise: The ABCDEs of planting a Freedom Church in Randyland

You might not be ready to go out and set up shop for the revolution in Randyland tomorrow, but it never hurts to start brainstorming. In this exercise, we'll take stock of your own neck of the woods and think through some opportunities and challenges there.

A: Assess *the terrain*

Even in your hometown, it can be hard to step back and assess the political, economic, social, and religious terrain clearly. Ask yourself: What is life actually like on the ground for the vast majority of people in White Christian nationalism–controlled regions of the country? How many people on the ground are actually represented by the political movement of White Christian nationalism that's taken hold of their power structure? Do they see themselves as aligned with it, served by it, empowered by it? Or do they see themselves being hurt by it? Or left out?

B: Be *strategic about religion*

Feel however salty you need to feel about religion; you've probably got plenty of valid reasons! But don't miss the opportunities that come with organizing with and through faith communities. Ask yourself: What resources do your local faith communities, including churches, have to offer the struggle for justice? Meeting space? Legal expertise? Contacts with local press?

And then ask yourself: Is there a church out there that might be primed to become a Freedom Church? If not, is there one pastor, lay leader, or badass congregation member who gets shit done and who you can conspire with? Or maybe there's a space where you can build your own Freedom Church. An empty mainline church building just waiting to be relevant? A food bank? Are there a handful of pissed-off, resourced Christians in your area who can give you a little seed funding to get started?

C: Come and meet Randy where he's at (and be consistent)

Gather a like-minded crew around you: others who are seeking to address local people's material needs while also asking big-picture questions about how best to counter the influence of White Christian nationalism. This could be your church, your book group, your football team. But it cannot be you alone. You need a squad.

Identify just one or two critical needs your team could organize to help folks meet: maybe handing out sack lunches once a week, or assisting folks with laundry at the laundromat. Whatever you identify, it is critical that you show up consistently; this is how you build trust.

Now, SHUT UP AND LISTEN. You should be listening 70 percent of the time at least and talking no more than 30 percent of the time. Emphasize hospitality and nonjudgment of the folks you meet as often as possible. The streets of Randyland—and indeed, all of White Christian nationalism's strongholds—tend to be mean-ass places toward the poor.

Always pair your material support with some kind of educational component: this could be a social justice Bible study, a movie night, or some other accessible, popular form of education.

As you start to accrue some regulars, make sure those regulars get involved in the leadership of the project: the logistics, helping to lead discussions and plan sessions, etc.

D: Don't be surprised if your outpost grows fast

If you're meeting key needs, if you're consistent, and if you're creating the kind of environment where struggling people feel safe, seen, and respected, well, people are gonna come. So, be ready to grow. Support the leadership and initiative of folks who show up and are willing and able to carry the work. Don't get petty and territorial over roles. We need as many folks as we can recruit.

E. Engage *a wider movement*

Find ways to start linking your little hub to a wider network. This could be the Freedom Church of the Poor network with the Kairos Center for Religions, Rights & Social Justice. Or it could be with the Poor People's Campaign: A National Call for Moral Revival. Or it could be a whole host of other national bodies committed to organizing poor and working people.

9

Rule Nine: Pledge Allegiance to the Bottom

I didn't grow up thinking politicians were particularly helpful or any good at getting things done. My grandma got things done, and my grandpa helped her. This was how the world ran according to little Aaron. In my mind as a child, my grandparents ran their neighborhood: they fed people, they cleared away the snow, they got the news, and they spread the news themselves. They did not wait for anyone else to come do this for them—not for ideological reasons but for practical ones. They simply couldn't wait forever. If you had a rare sighting of a politician in public somewhere, it was eventful in the same way that seeing a soap opera star is eventful. Exciting the way the circus is exciting.

My grandma moved to the United States from Scotland when she was twenty, trading the industrial slums of Dundee for the peak era of America's imperial economy. She was coming from one of the most militant working-class, women-run labor cities on earth, and in fact, she hailed from an even older lineage of poor people's organizing than this. One of my favorite accounts of that lineage is this one, about the Scottish cattle-rustling border clans, courtesy of that fount of wisdom, Wikipedia:

> The difficulty and uncertainties of basic human survival meant that communities and/or people kindred to each other would seek security through group strength and cunning. They would attempt to improve their livelihoods at their nominal enemies' expense, enemies who were frequently also just trying to survive. Loyalty to a feeble or distant monarch and reliance on the effectiveness of the law usually made people a target for depredations rather than conferring any security.

> These borderers proved difficult to control . . . They were already in the habit of claiming any nationality or none, depending on who was asking and where they perceived the individual advantage to be. Many had relatives on both sides . . . despite prevailing laws against international marriage . . . As warriors more loyal to clans than to nations, their commitment . . . was always in doubt.

That was Grandma to a T. If the choices are between holding my breath for a legislator to show up and be helpful in a working-class neighborhood and something like clan loyalty, give me "security through group strength and cunning" any day!

What does my grandma's lineage have to do with Randy and with fighting White Christian nationalism, exactly? For starters, it's because of Grandma that I understand loyalty deeply and nationalism not at all.

This might sound abstract or even nonsensical to you, but it's not. The propaganda machine of White Christian nationalism plays hard on "loyalty to America" tropes. If you don't rely every single day on networks of loyalty for your material and social survival, you probably don't understand why this kind of messaging presses a lot of buttons for people.

There's plenty to say about how "loyalty" is a concept badly used and abused to control people: in families, in faith communities, in workplaces, everywhere. Nobody should feel like they need to be "loyal" to someone or some system that's exploiting and abusing them.

At the same time, I don't know why, but most of the progressives I've been around seem almost as allergic to talking about the positive and useful aspects of loyalty as they are allergic to talking about the positive and useful aspects of religion. Maybe it's a class thing, and most progressives haven't relied on ties of loyalty for their personal survival? Or maybe it's an academia thing, and somehow loyalty is out of fashion because it comes across as "uncritical"?

I don't actually know why anyone else thinks what they think. All I know is that my own experience has taught me that all of us are choosing our loyalties as we make our way through life; some of us just delude ourselves into believing we're freer agents than we think.

Loyalty—allegiance—is about who you're willing to ride for, even in the bad times. And it's about who is willing to ride for you in the bad times. We're in some damn bad times right now. People are finding out who's really here for them. And people are finding out who they are really here for.

Who are you really here for? Who's really here for you: when you get fired, when your kid's in the hospital, when you need to get out of an abusive home, when you're ready to quit drinking but you don't know what to do next?

For most people in this country, the honest version of that list is pretty short: maybe a couple relatives, a couple friends. In many other countries, there's this crazy idea that all society should have your back in those moments of crisis, because it turns out that masses of sick, desperate, suffering people are a very destabilizing reality. But this is America. So, for Randy, when it all hits the fan, he's probably just gonna call you. No wonder your Aunt Barb is sick of his shit. In Nigeria or Bolivia or Finland or Vietnam, there'd be an entire community, village, or social welfare system helping her pick up the slack.

It's simply too much for one tired-ass auntie to carry alone.

We all believe stories about something

It's shit like this that makes me appreciate being anchored in a faith tradition. Why? Because a faith tradition gives me the opportunity to deeply know and trust and live into stories that are older than the United States. Older than capitalism. Older than that toxic rugged individualism bullshit.

Yes, Christianity is crusty and problematic AF, but I personally do not ever get tired of hearing a story about God taking sides with the poor. I never get tired of hearing about God asking to be born to a poor mom on the run. And then she says yes, and so God is born as a tiny homeless baby who grows up to give away free medical care and food and education. And God goes on to call out the powerful for abusing the lowly, as one born among the lowly, until the day the empire comes to string God up. But even then, they can't keep this revolutionary God, this revolutionary love, in the ground? Sign me up for that story. Every single time.

Too many segments* of contemporary American Christianity—especially the kind inclined toward justice and liberation—don't leverage this story the way we could. Our faith traditions and holy texts are a powerful way to remind ourselves and one another just how screwed up, illogical, barbaric, and sinful this society we've inherited really is—and that there are other ways to live, and that maybe even God wants us to reorganize this shit from the ground up. The Bible itself is full of stories of people at the very bottom of society being chosen by God to lead. Not just in a woo-woo spiritual way but to lead social, political, and economic movements of leveling unjust structures and building new and better ones.

I can hear you thinking, "Stories? You're gonna fight White Christian nationalism by telling Bible stories? WTF? What about all the actually useful things like voting?!"

By all means, go vote. Elections are one tool in a belt containing thousands of tools; we should use them according to their purpose and scale. But if we are genuinely seeking justice for all people and indeed the whole of creation, we have to get real that participating in elections will never let us off the hook for mass civil disobedience, direct action, political education, organizing, and oppressed people taking back land and the

---

* I won't say this is exclusively a shortcoming of White mainline churches, but I also won't . . . not say it.

175

means of production. It didn't take four years for this country to reach its current state; it took four hundred. What we are seeing now, what has been coming all along, is the fall of the American empire.

The Roman Empire that lynched Jesus ran for about four hundred years before it entered its one-hundred-year fall. Religious people, if we're paying attention to our own backstory, are predisposed to thinking in this sort of timeline much more than a four-year election cycle. Some Christians in America might have forgotten the really important parts of this, given all the White Christian nationalism in our groundwater. But we've kinda got this whole thing about a God who was killed by a brutal empire. Most Sundays in church, we read about empires collapsing. You'd think we'd have been a little more prepared for it to happen in real time, but alas. A lot of us have been comfortably propping up our institutions, maybe with a little tweak here and there, not fundamentally wondering when the foundations will start to shake.

That's another thing about empires: they undo themselves, in the end. We expose our own arrogance when we believe we control when and how the foundations will shake, because this empire does not belong to regular people. It does not serve us. It does not work for us. What we can do, here on the ground, is understand the signs, know the collapse is coming (even when those in power would rather have us look the other way), and prepare ourselves and our communities to get up and run toward forty years in the wilderness.

What are the signs of imperial collapse? Sheesh, take your pick from the headlines today. Endless wars abroad, with the most sophisticated and expensive death machines money can buy, while kids at home go hungry and you can't even count the number of people sleeping under bridges anymore. A political "leadership" class that's morally and intellectually bankrupt on both sides of the aisle, with no real accountability to the electorate. Escalating social violence. The list goes on. And as an empire collapses, more and more people end up on the bottom. Those of us who are already poor today are just the canaries in the coal mine for what's coming more broadly. As the climate changes, as inequality tips ever wider, and as social and political systems break down, we who are poor are living today what you, if you're not poor, might be living tomorrow. Remember: your future is Randy's present.

So what moves do we make during the collapse of the next one hundred years? How will we organize to fill new voids of power in a way that serves the poor and the oppressed, knowing we are not the only forces seeking to fill that void? How do we start thinking and dreaming at the scale of decades, like our adversaries at the First Church of White Christian Nationalism, rather than in four-year election cycles?

Know what helps us start to imagine time on that scale? Stories do. BIBLE stories.

Loyalty to the bottom

"Can anything good come out of Nazareth?" Some of you Bible-thumpers reading this book will recognize that from the first chapter of the Gospel of John. For the rest of you, this book's almost over, so just let me preach.

Nazareth was Jesus's hometown, and it was a rough place. Randy would've fit right in. It was also a place where people pledged their allegiance to their kin and their neighbors rather than to the brutal, colonizing Roman imperial army.

Asking "Can anything good come out of Nazareth?" is a lot like asking, "Can anything good come out of the trailer park?" Out of the rez? The projects? The county jail? The trap?

Archaeologist Yardenna Alexandre has done several excavations in Nazareth. These excavations are not just within the contemporary city limits but within the very small area of the village of Nazareth that existed during the early Roman Empire: the Nazareth of Mary, the Nazareth of Jesus.

Nazareth was not an important place at this time. It wasn't on the roads. Likewise, the people of Galilee, and of Nazareth in particular, were not considered important; the Jewish families who ended up there were families who had been displaced from Jerusalem. Who couldn't compete with the pressure for land there and were dumped off by the Hasmonean Empire, which pushed them out to settle in some isolated backwater. Alexandre says the history shows there was a lot of unemployment among these families, a lot of conflict, a lot of struggle for daily survival. In a July 2020 interview, Alexandre described her findings and said, "people didn't go through Nazareth unless they specifically wanted to go there"—because it wasn't on the way to anything.

At her dig sites, Alexandre found a whole system of dug-out pits dating back to the Iron Age. The pits were made by hewing out the soft chalk bedrock underneath the homes of ancient Nazareth, and they were storage pits: for water, for grapes, for oil, all of that. But she found something more than that. Beneath the first level of these dug-out units, there was usually a second level to the pit . . . and then sometimes a third, altogether going about sixteen feet down. Then some of the dug-out units in each household connected to units in other households through an extensive series of underground tunnels—even though, during that era, people were living their daily lives above ground.

So, what were the hidden underground pits and tunnels for? Alexandre says they served two purposes. People used these pits to escape and to hide from the Roman army. And get this: Yardenna Alexandre says that the hidden levels of the pits allowed families in Nazareth to practice extensive tax evasion from the Roman Empire.

The empire was taking too much from the people (what's new!). The people needed to survive, and so they hid a significant amount of their produce, their harvest, whatever crops they had that Rome would take in taxes. She says that based on the dating of the pits, we know that this was a widespread and common practice in Nazareth at the time of the annunciation—when Mary learned from the angel Gabriel that she would become a mother—and throughout the lifetime of Jesus. It more than likely happened in Mary and Jesus's own home.

So, Jesus is not only born in a poor, rural, isolated backwater. Jesus is born into a community of shrewd hustlers.

When God sends the angel Gabriel to a household where people are breaking the law in order to survive, God essentially tells Gabriel, "That's where you will find the young woman I am looking for, the One to whom I'm entrusting my life." It's worth noting that the earth beneath the Basilica of the Annunciation is absolutely packed with these units. Almost as if Mary were the literal queen bee of this underground economy.

So, these are Jesus's people. This is Jesus's family. This is the place that shapes Jesus's mind, identity, and early orientation to the world. And this, I think, is exactly what Nathanael is asking about in John 1:46 when he asks, "Can anything good come out of Nazareth?"

Can anything good come out of a people so hard-pressed that they're all committing crimes of survival, all on the wrong side of the law because they'd rather feed their families than fall in line? Can anything worthy come from a place where everyone melts into the hillside when the police show up?

This history speaks so immediately to the reality and the spirituality of the congregation that sprouted up at our rural Freedom Church of the Poor in Grays Harbor. Ours was a church of the streets, the camps, the cellblocks, and the flophouses.

I think most nice church people understood us as a ministry of charity because we did a lot of charitable stuff: constantly feeding, sheltering, clothing, and pastoring people. But the basic equation most people assume is that we did this work in a place and among a people with only despair and lack to offer. A gaping hole of need.

And certainly, despair and lack are present; there are generations of poverty, generations of trauma. But as with Nazareth, there are also generations of resistance to the imperial order. And I'm not talking about respectable, righteous-sounding, or attention-grabbing kinds of resistance—not particularly notable marches with highbrow speakers. I'm talking about the kind of resistance that poor people always mount under empire, because poor people's survival always demands disobedience to interests of the rich and powerful.

In our congregation, we pastored people who made their homes by digging out tunnels in the earth in order to hide from the police because their poverty placed them on the wrong side of the law. Just about everyone in our parish had a criminal record. Just about everyone had been banned from Walmart for theft. Just about everyone had been involved in the street economy—trading in stolen goods, or drugs, or sex—because those were the economic opportunities to which they had access.

People choose survival even when their survival is made illegal. And there is nothing glamorous or romantic about that reality. But it is incredibly clarifying. It exposes all the lies we tell in this society about equality, about liberty and justice for all, about our government fundamentally valuing us. Under empire—including the US empire—we are all varying degrees of disposable.

Poor people are never allowed to forget this. And yet poor people choose to live anyway. Even when it is a crime. Even when they risk being beaten bloody by the police for stealing food from Safeway, people choose to assert their right to life. Even when told the lie that poverty strips them of the fitness to parent, people choose to raise children—like Mary did. And people find ways to provide for their children, even when it's illegal—like Mary did.

I think about God scanning the map, deciding where to send the angel Gabriel to announce God's planned arrival, when Nazareth comes into focus. God needs to be born someplace off the beaten path that won't attract much attention. God needs to grow up in a place where the way of the people is to choose life regardless of whether the power structure says they are entitled to life. And God—in the soft, warm, completely vulnerable body of a newborn human—needs provision despite the odds.

There is Nazareth, and right in the middle of it—at the center of the underground hive of oil, wheat, and wine that the people have taken back for themselves—is Mary's house. I imagine God chooses her residence because it is the most comfortably stocked with stolen merchandise: so full that she is able to share with all her neighbors. "Yes," God says when Mary comes into focus, "She's the one." Hail Mary, Queen of Thieves. Hail Mary, Queen of Daily Bread. A queen for those at the bottom, with no allegiance to the top.

Anytime poor people come together with that level of organization and collaboration in the service of collective survival, God is bound to be born in the midst of it.

Exercise: Your own pledge of allegiance

Take some time to answer the following questions:

* Who (individuals, groups, communities) are you loyal to, even in hard times?
* What (ideals, beliefs, organizations, institutions) are you loyal to, even in hard times?
* How is your loyalty earned? How have you earned the loyalty of others?
* What does this loyalty cost you? What does it cost others?
* How does this loyalty strengthen and sustain you? How does it strengthen and sustain others?

Now take a minute to write your own (honest) pledge of allegiance. After you've written it, read it and reflect on it. Is this a pledge that lives up to your values and commitments? Where would you like to see it be stronger? What parts of it feel strong already?

10

Rule Ten: Never Forget
That the Revolution Comes
to Randyland Too

It's getting late in this book. Allow me to preach for just a little bit longer.

The Bible says Jesus was crucified between two thieves— three cons in a row strung up together, and the one in the middle just happens to be God Incarnate. That's really all we hear about those guys, and a detail like that dropped in a story ("this one's a thief, and that one is too") is usually enough to enable us to coolly distance ourselves from their reality.

But here's the thing: empire makes thieves of us all. None of us have clean hands in this sin-sick society—not you, not me, not Randy, and certainly not any of the people with more power than we've got.

If we're not selling drugs, we're selling our labor dirt cheap to multinational corporations, or forking over all our money to them because we need food, we need health care, we need medicine. If you aren't sitting behind bars, the food on your plate was probably picked by children—and if you are sitting behind bars, you likely don't even recognize what's on the plate in front of you. This economic system does not offer us any choices untainted with the blood of the poor and the destruction of the earth.

But just like the Roman Empire did to the thieves who died on either side of Jesus, our own empire stays busy locking up poor people who are labeled thieves for trying to survive. They don't lock up the thieves on Wall Street. Or the thieves who steal voting rights. Or the thieves who made money hand over fist by cashing in their stocks when they first caught wind of what the pandemic would bring in its wake.

Because we live in an empire, both of our major political parties are ultimately beholden to exploitive, violent, imperial interests. One party masks this somewhat, and the other party does not. The success of every empire hinges on its ability to divide and conquer.

And divide and conquer isn't just a military operation; it's an ideological operation. This is where imperial co-opting of religion becomes so critical. We know that Jesus was killed by the Roman Empire in a manner of execution reserved specifically for rebel slaves. We encounter in the Bible long, fraught diatribes against empire and against the concentration of wealth, land, and power.

And yet, the birth of my own denomination, the Episcopal Church, in this country is inseparable from the transatlantic slave trade. The Jamestown Colony in Virginia, the site of the first holy communion service in North America, was also the site to which the first kidnapped Africans were taken on this continent as a replacement labor force for the 80 percent of European indentured servants the Virginia Company starved to death in the colony in 1609 and 1610. This same site of death and exploitation was the site of the very first election, held in the first church on this continent. The wealth and power born in that sin endures in my denomination today. Trinity Episcopal Church on Wall Street, founded by the colonial ruling class in 1696 and physically built by Black people who were enslaved by wealthy White congregation members, manages real estate properties that had a combined worth of over $6 billion as of 2019.

This is a staggering legacy to consider. It's beyond sobering to look clearly at the legacies of our society's institutions across the political spectrum and find that again, and again, and again, we cannot outrun the original sins of this nation's founding.

But maybe what can keep us grounded and keep us going is the knowledge that there are other legacies to hold on to too.

The American imperial project, corrupted from the beginning by the sins of genocide and captivity, has also been resisted powerfully since the very beginning. When my wife and I visited Jamestown a few years ago, we drove near the Great Dismal Swamp. For ten generations, from the colonization of Jamestown to the end of the Civil War, the Great Dismal Swamp was a destination and a permanently organized community: for Indigenous people fleeing the encroaching frontier, for African people fleeing enslavement, and for indentured White servants fleeing the law. People raised crops and livestock and sunflowers in the swamp. They set up their own governance and held their own religious life centered on African spiritual practices—for ten generations! This was a literal Exodus-to-the-wilderness story, happening right in the belly of the imperial beast.

We aren't far from having to figure out how to face our own wilderness; indeed, many of us are already in it. This empire continues to rot. That's a frightening thing. But we know from our history that revolutionary possibility, transformation, and the power of the poor all meet us in the wilderness.

The solution to Moses and the Hebrews' troubles with Pharaoh wasn't to elect a kinder, gentler Pharaoh; it was about breaking Pharaoh's system by getting free from it. The fight over chattel slavery in this country wasn't about implementing a kinder, gentler plantation system; it was about abolition. In each era of history, the solution is to pull together leaders from the bottom of the imperial order in pursuit of radical transformation. Our task is to remember that truth, nurture that truth, and build up leaders who will defend and live that truth anew for generations to come.

Things are getting worse out there. It's important to accept this—not as a permanent and irreversible truth but as a sober and grounded analysis of how to meet the moment. We don't yet have the fighting movement we need to turn this ship around. We can build it (indeed, we already are). But we need to be strong enough to build it in worsening conditions over the next generation, with a clear understanding of the kind of power and strategy and commitment it will really take to change the direction we're heading in.

Remember that mainline church in my hometown that's now home to a classical Christian academy? Here's another true story of an old mainline church with a dwindling congregation, one that made a different choice than the church in my hometown that gave itself over to the Doug Wilson crowd. It demonstrates another possibility.

The right kind of wrong people

When we started Chaplains on the Harbor, the bishop let us take over an old church building. The previous congregation had shrunk to four worshippers on Sunday—three of whom were serving on the altar, so do the math as far as how many people were in the pews—when they finally decided to call it quits.

My co-pastor Cedar and I were both navigating the ordination process in the Episcopal denomination at the time, and we were looking for a building we could use in our emerging Freedom Church of the Poor. Both from small, hard-up, rural, predominantly White towns, we knew the transformational impact that a local, multiracial movement–centered community space could have.

We met with that small congregation in this process, and they shared how hard it had been to draw people to the church—especially young people. But then their sole remaining Sunday attendee told us this: "I just hope you don't let those homeless people put their tents on the church property."

Evidently young people without housing weren't the kind of young people they'd been looking for. But they were precisely who we, as the Freedom Church of the Poor, were seeking.

We ended up sorely disappointing that last remaining church member. Soon enough, we were being inundated by young homeless people. They'd show up at the church each day as soon as the doors were open. This was for communal, spiritual, and political reasons as much as it was for material and survival reasons. We had free coffee and Wi-Fi, and we had a weekly political education program called The School of Hard Knocks. We had free meals and winter shelter, and we hosted organizers from poor communities across the country to come exchange lessons with us.

We had staff to offer harm reduction supplies, clergy to accompany people on their court dates, and posters on the wall explaining, with graphs and illustrations, the last fifty years of cuts to the federal housing budget. Sometimes people would ask one of the pastors to pray with them, or to perform a wedding, or to visit their girlfriend in jail. Nobody got converted, but everybody got fed. Everybody had a chance to share their skills and expertise. Everybody had a chance to study and learn.

At first, we didn't really have any funding. We started with a $500 grant, a backpack full of sandwiches, and a pack of cigarettes.* The institutional church was, initially, a very slow and grudging supporter. But we were patient, and we were relentless, and people kept coming, and we kept growing.

Within just a few years, we were the fifth largest congregation in the diocese, and we could no longer be ignored. We could no longer be told that what we were doing was impossible, unviable, unsustainable. Were we ever financially solvent?† Absolutely not; we were a congregation of six hundred poor,

---

* Smoking is bad for you. But offering someone a cigarette is an excellent, short-hand way of communicating a certain level of non-judgment— especially with people who are being judged constantly.

† If I had a dollar for all the times we were grilled about financial "sustainability" by the institutional church, I would be financially sustainable. The mainline church asks this question before all others. Our idolatry of the market is shameless.

homeless, and incarcerated people. Did we keep pushing the work forward anyway? Yes.

The story of these two churches—the one from my hometown that caved, and the one that sprang up from the streets of Grays Harbor County—poses a most pressing question for churches truly seeking to wade into the struggle to counter White Christian nationalism: Which young people do you seek? Young families who can afford $10,000 a year in private Christian school tuition? Or young families struggling to survive? Young professionals with lots of options and resources and wealth? Or young people who have been kicked out by their parents for being queer or who can't find an apartment with rent cheap enough to afford on a job that pays them $15 an hour?

Sharing what you have (like a big old church building) with one of these groups will keep your bills paid. Sharing what you have with the other is the example that Jesus commanded us to follow.

Churches: Which side are you on?

In this particular moment of history, with the ascendancy of White Christian nationalism so undeniable, a church or a nonprofit or an individual deciding that they can dabble in the fight against fascism only when it's financially convenient to do so is delusional as well as sinful. My mentor Willie Baptist says it best: "Nobody's gonna pay you to kick their ass."

There isn't any neutral ground left to stand on (not that it ever existed in the first place). Eventually, if you're with a church, the choice comes knocking on the door of your congregation, whether you like it or not. At that point, you will have one of three choices:

1. Sell your space to the encroaching private Christian school, right-wing church plant, or real estate developer, with the deal that you can still hang on to one little corner to meet on Sunday;

2. Close up shop because you can't cover expenses and can't imagine a new way forward (the Christian school/megachurch/real estate developer/corporation will pounce anyway, now that you're out of their way); or

3. Dig deep—I mean really deep, rock bottom deep—into the material suffering in your community, remembering that your community does not stop at the edge of your congregation.

Remember I said I was going to get preachy? So don't say I didn't warn you. Let me tell you what to do: choose number three. Pitch a vision of church with the poorest people in your neighborhood at the center of it: as full participants, as leaders, as teachers. Know that there will be people in your congregation, your denomination, and your neighborhood who will fight you on this tooth and nail. They will tell you that it's too risky, that it's not financially sustainable. You can remind them that the gospel doesn't teach much about risk-aversion or fiscal stability, and meanwhile, White Christian nationalists are snatching up Randys and real estate all across America. Cede nothing. The stakes are too high. Pledge your allegiance to the poor and dispossessed and let this be the foundation upon which we build our movement to uproot White Christian nationalism.

Poor and working people across this country have been so hurt by the church. There are a lot of profoundly faithful folks you couldn't pay to darken the door of a church because of the ways they've been shamed, blamed, and judged for their own suffering—or because they've been given the most superficial, warped, manipulative justifications for their suffering. There are millions of people out there longing for a spiritual community, people who will tell you they're gun-shy because they've had bad experiences at church.

What I have found over the course of organizing as a faith leader for the last twenty years is this: those bad experiences are almost always tied to White Christian nationalism in some way. From violently homophobic sermons, to having to listen to hate speech against at Christian feeding programs, to propping up and protecting abusers of power, the very worst of White Christian nationalism is blaring at full volume in countless far-right churches across the country every Sunday. But this happens plenty of times in moderate, liberal, and progressive churches too, whenever the maintenance of wealth and status comes at the sacrifice of justice for poor and oppressed people. The same church that passionately devotes its resources, education, and volunteer work toward climate change and holiday food drives for the homeless will frequently struggle to connect the dots when homeless leaders show up in need of support and protection from climate change's effects after their encampment floods. Poor people feel betrayed by the church so often because they heard this story about a guy who went around giving out free food and health care two thousand years ago—and they expected more of the institutions claiming to follow him.

This is not to say struggling people show up at a church expecting their every need to be met. But they do expect more than platitudes, and they certainly expect more than judgment. Perversely, sometimes the churches more aligned with White Christian nationalism are better at standing in this gap than churches in the liberal mainline.

A new Moral Majority

I've spent a lot of time with people who use lots of drugs (or who did, once upon a time). There are around six hundred people in our Redneck Freedom Church of the Poor scattered across the county's encampments, back alleys, jail cells, and trailer parks. I love my people, and therefore I despise the ways a very superficial, distorted notion of "morality" has been used to bludgeon them with blame, with self-loathing, with state and vigilante violence at every turn.

It's time to reexamine our notions of "morality"—and to help Randy do the same.

Poor people are relentlessly scapegoated and pathologized as being wasteful, immoral, licentious, and intemperate. Poor people are convenient scapegoats for our lethally imbalanced political and economic system. Media coverage of the 2020 uprisings in the wake of the highly publicized police murders of Breonna Taylor, Tony McDade, and George Floyd sharply illuminate this point. Hand-wringing moderates, usually of some economic stability, clutch their pearls and gasp, "Protesting is one thing, but looting is unacceptable!"

Why? This country has been looting poor people since day one. America has particularly looted poor Black people of bodily autonomy, of labor, of wealth, of political power, of family, of safety, of health, of life itself in an ongoing history of atrocities. Even in my broke-ass redneck parish, responding to the prolific misinformation that "looters" might attempt to come to our community, my co-pastor simply replied, "Capitalism and the timber industry looted Aberdeen a long time ago. There is nothing left to take."

In the void left by timber, Aberdeen saw the emergence of incarceration as a replacement industry—both in the form of a state prison used to incarcerate Black and Brown people from other poor communities and as an expansion of municipal and county jails to incarcerate local poor White and Indigenous people. In tandem with the expansion of policing, criminalization, and incarceration, we have seen an absolute explosion of the drug economy.

Drugs do not flood poor communities in the United States by accident, and they never have. It is not an accident that the small city at the epicenter of opioid overdoses in Washington State for decades lacked an inpatient treatment program. It is not an accident that this town of sixteen thousand people, with one thousand people homeless, apparently cannot fund affordable housing but can always find the resources to secure more militarized police equipment. Likewise, it is not an accident that the dominant local narrative around addiction is inseparably intertwined with the local narrative around poverty: bootstrap your way out of it. If you can't—if for some ungodly reason you need help, health care, housing, meaningful living-wage work before you can heal—then you are weak, dissolute, and should be consumed with shame. At the end of the day, this is the formula for "morality" that White Christian nationalism offers to poor people.

And what is the "morality" we have permitted billion-dollar corporations and the rich to have? *Here, have some more. Of everything. Have another formerly working-class neighborhood to gentrify while homeless people are dying in the streets. Have another round of water rights while Flint's taps still run with poison. Have another war over oil while veteran rates of suicide skyrocket. Have*

*another city council or key senator's seat in your pocket while poor
people are disenfranchised through escalating voter suppression.*

"This system treats injuries to the rich as public crises
requiring massive government action, but injuries to the rest of
us as the unfortunate results of bad luck and personal moral
failures," writes Shailly Gupta Barnes, policy director of the Poor
People's Campaign: A National Call for Moral Revival. "It is able
to do this—and sustain this inequality—through the creation
and reinforcement of the powerful ideological belief that an
economy that benefits the rich will benefit the rest of us."

You, Randy, and I are currently living through one of the
most violent and volatile moments of human history. We live in
a society whose economy and politics are fundamentally structured around maintaining the power of the most wealthy. In the
first ten weeks of the pandemic, US billionaire wealth increased
by $485 billion, while forty million Americans filed for unem-
ployment. Prior to the coronavirus outbreak, nearly half of
Americans were already poor or low-wealth. So, what might true
morality look like in this moment of American public life?

The only theologically sound definition of morality we can
pursue at this point in human history must be a revolutionary
morality. This morality must be collective, and it must be structural. In the days to come, we need a new morality—a new
"moral majority," you might say. So, what does morality look
like in a society already at war with the poor and oppressed, with
conflict steadily spreading and escalating?

We must first and foremost seek material morality—
concrete balance, mercy, and hospitality—in our distribution of
political and economic power. In June 2019, the Poor People's
Campaign released the "Poor People's Moral Budget," identifying

enormous sources of financial and political redress for the 140 million Americans who are poor or one emergency away from poverty, including: $350 billion in annual military spending cuts; $886 billion in estimated annual revenue from fair taxes on the wealthy, corporations, and Wall Street; and billions more in savings from ending mass incarceration, addressing climate change, and meeting other key campaign demands.

Second: we will need the moral center in our strategy. By "moral center," I do not mean centrism; just the opposite. We are faced with the reality of immediate, critical, mass life-and-death struggles. We have to meet this reality with the utmost urgency, while at the same time recognizing that our current layers of crisis are centuries in the making and will not be undone quickly. Rome wasn't built in a day, and neither did it fall in a day. Our movement to restore balance, restore justice, restore right relationships with one another and the whole of creation will be, by necessity, the project of generations. We need the kind of morality, fortitude, and endurance that will allow us to run a long game, constantly and effectively recruiting more and more people into what the Reverend Dr. Martin Luther King Jr. once called "the nonviolent army of the poor."

Third: We are in a *kairos* moment in history right now. *Kairos* is an ancient Greek word that refers to a time that is outside of chronological time—an opportune moment, a time ordained and provisioned. This kairos time requires of us a profound spiritual grounding. We are outgunned. We are outspent. We have numbers on our side in terms of the numbers of people who are suffering from poverty, violence, and repression, but we are not yet nearly organized enough to contend directly with the forces we're up against.

The scale and scope of what we face is staggering, and despair over the hope of our cause is a real and chronic specter. And yet, this has always been true for poor people under empire. Empires have always fallen. Empires eventually do themselves in, in the end—in new and horrifying ways each time, but with great consistency nonetheless.

What is never a given is what—and who—will emerge from the rubble.

This part is, in many ways, our responsibility. Laboring to bring a new world forth from this rubble is a deeply intellectual commitment, a deeply political commitment, and an even more deeply spiritual commitment. What kind of movement can meet this task? What kind of spirituality?

Randy is one key to unlocking this kairos movement. Right now, if he's on the radar at all, he's usually being treated like White Christian nationalism's pawn. He is robbed of true political agency to address the root causes of his suffering and shape the conditions of his life. He needs to be won over—hard—and brought into a movement that sees him, that loves him, that accepts him and challenges him to see further and more expansively: who he is, who is really on this side, and who isn't.

The movement that helps us go get Randy and then embraces him when he shows up takes many forms, from the poor-organizing-the-poor models of the National Union of the Homeless and the Nonviolent Medicaid Army to the justice-not-judgment street chaplaincy of Rev. Lindsey Krinks in Nashville.

I have had the immense gift of witnessing the spirit of this movement already at work in the daily lives of countless poor people. This is the kind of spirit that doggedly anchors itself in life and human connection through songs shouted through the drains, through love letters to the outside, even during lockdown at the county jail. This is the kind of spirit that drives someone to socialize their entire month's worth of food stamps in order to share a feast with twenty other homeless people. True spiritual power is not only self-sacrifice; it is also deep inner orientation to finding and enacting balance in the face of excess. When every excess you face is an excess of deprivation and lack, the spiritual counter to this will very often look like trusting in and mimicking the abundance of God.

In the material, strategic, and spiritual means called for in this revolutionary moment, then, let's move forward together. We can be wise as serpents and innocent as doves, as Jesus said. We can pop off like Jesus in the midst of the money changers in the temple, turning over tables, swatting away their plans to enrich themselves, and getting all up in the faces of people who are taking advantage of the poor. Now that's truly the kind of movement Randy can bang with.

Exercise: Say a little prayer for Randy

Look, I don't care if you're not religious. Randy needs you, and you need him, and we all need both of y'all. And when you want to give something (like a relationship, or a commitment, or a movement) power and reverence and life, you need to feed it some intentional words.

So let him hear it. Say a prayer for Randy. You can do this on your own or in a place he can hear you. If you don't like the word *prayer*, you can swap it out for *poem* or *love letter*, or you can write him a damn classic rock ballad. If it works, get on the phone and call him, just to genuinely ask how he's doing. Find the means to communicate to him that he's important to you. You love him, and you're rooting for him, and you're not giving up on him despite this cruel and messed-up country.

Now look in the mirror and say the same damn thing to yourself.

I'm not crying, you're crying.

Keep your head up.

ACKNOWLEDGMENTS

Thank you to my lineage—especially to my grandparents Ivy and Leland Scott. The lives you lived continue to be better guides to me than any book or teacher.

Thank you to my sister Kelly, for getting me off my ass and making me take this project seriously, and also to my brother-in-law, Kris, and my nephews, Miles and Avery, for letting us move into your basement for a year so we didn't have to sell the truck while I wrote this book.

Thank you to my mom for hanging that "Jesus is LORD" cross-stitch right next to your "UNION STRONG" poster. You get it.

Thank you to my best friend and cofounder Cedar Monroe. I'm so glad we've both lived to tell these tales. I wasn't always sure that we would, haha!

Thank you to my cousin Emily Nilsson, for inspiring more salty cracker jokes than anyone on earth. This book is a lot funnier thanks to you.

Thank you to all my mentors in this work, first and foremost Willie Baptist and Rev. Dr. Liz Theoharis. You two have taught me (and continue to teach me) everything important I know about organizing.

Thank you to my readers: Maria Cervini, Kelly Scott, Rev. Dr. Liz Theoharis, Cedar Monroe, Emily Nilsson, Carol Lautier, Rev. Dr. Jessica Williams, and my beautiful editorial prince Noam Sandweiss-Back.

Thank you to my editor, Valerie Weaver-Zercher, at Broadleaf, for giving me time and so much encouragement to sit and sift through the episode of *Hoarders* that is my brain. I've never once been able to pay attention to a project this long; the credit all goes to you for pulling it off.

Thank you from the bottom of my heart to all the teachers I've ever had the privilege of getting to know through Chaplains on the Harbor. Rest in peace and rise in power to my countless friends on the Harbor gone too soon. Deep gratitude to the movement family across the country; you have witnessed and supported our work on the ground, and you have welcomed us into your own communities and struggles.

Thank you above all to my beautiful wife, Rev. Erica Williams Scott, who encouraged, agitated, inspired, challenged, and celebrated this project every step of the way. It's not an exaggeration to say that I would not have finished this without you. I love you. Your turn now.

Finally, thank you to Moses—my kind, fair, funny, strong, fast, and wise kid—who makes the fight for a better world worth facing every day. I'm so proud of you, Dreamkeeper. Love, Dada.

NOTES

Introduction

4 ***80-or-so percent of us Americans who aren't straight, White, cis-gender Christian men:*** "The American Religious Landscape in 2020," Public Religion Research Institute, July 8, 2021, https://www.prri.org/research/2020-census-of-american-religion/. I had to guestimate the gender breakdown here, but women generally outrank men in rates of religious identity.

16 ***how-to manuals on the nuts and bolts of traditional organizing:*** See, for example, "Our Resources," Indivisible, accessed January 30, 2024, https://www.indivisible.org/resources.

Rule One: Come Get Your Cousin Randy

22 ***White Christian nationalism, at its core:*** For lots more detail on this, along with interviews from the front lines, see Kairos Center for Religions, Rights, and Social Justice and the MoveOn Education Fund, *All of U.S.: Organizing to Counter White Christian Nationalism and Build a Pro-Democracy Society,* May 2023, https://drive.google.com/file/d/1KIMmtfbVF2R27F4gpC61Bguo7jlp5cuU/view.

25 ***Those details are mostly beyond the scope of this book:*** For a great orientation to the MVPs in this network, see Katherine Stewart's *The Power Worshippers: Inside the Dangerous Rise of Religious Nationalism.* For an excellent ground-level view of it from inside the belly of a suburban megachurch, see Bradley Onishi's *Preparing for War: The*

Extremist History of White Christian Nationalism—And What Comes Next. For a thorough and historic tracing of the White supremacy that has shaped this contemporary movement over the past century, see Dr. Anthea Butler's *White Evangelical Racism.* For coverage of the historic, unholy marriage between big business and the church, see *One Nation Under God: How Corporate America Invented Christian America* by Kevin Kruse.

26 **more than a million dollars of pandemic aid back:** Dave Haviland, "Two Grays Harbor Commissioners Say No to Low-Barrier Shelter," *The Chronicle,* April 23, 2021, https://www.chronline.com/stories/two-grays-harbor-commissioners-say-no-to-low-barrier-shelter,262945.

32 **civil rights leader Ms. Ruby Sales's advice:** Ruby Sales, interview by Krista Tippett, "Where Does It Hurt?" *On Being Project,* September 15, 2016, https://onbeing.org/programs/ruby-sales-where-does-it-hurt/.

32 **civil rights mastermind Ella Baker:** "Ella Baker Organizes NAACP Chapters in the South," Digital SNCC Gateway, accessed January 15, 2024, https://snccdigital.org/events/ella-baker-organizes-naacp-chapters/.

32 **She had been working with the NAACP:** See *The Rebellious Life of Mrs. Rosa Parks* by Jeanne Theoharis (New York: Penguin Random House, 2013) for so much more.

Rule Two: Talk to Randy Like You Actually Give a Damn about Him

38 **Randyland holds vastly disproportionate sway:** Emily Badger, "As American as Apple Pie? The Rural Vote's Disproportionate Slice of Power," *New York Times,* November 20, 2016, https://www.nytimes.com/2016/11/21/upshot/as-american-as-apple-pie-the-rural-votes-disproportionate-slice-of-power.html.

44 **Wilson is famous both for enabling sexual abuse:** With a big trigger warning, see Rachel L. Shubin, "Analyzing Douglas Wilson's Handling of the Steven Sitler and Jamin Wight Cases," The Truth about Moscow, accessed January 30, 2024, https://www.moscowid.net/

wp-content/uploads/2016/09/Analyzing-DWs-Response-to-Sitler-and-Wight-Cases.pdf.

44 *"slavery produced in the South a genuine affection":* Steve Wilkins and Douglas Wilson, *Southern Slavery as It Was* (Moscow, ID: Cannon Press, 1996), https://susannalee.org/courses/print/Wilkins-Wilson_1996-print.pdf.

46 *Turning Point USA alone currently has a budget of:* Matthew Boedy, "Ten Years of Turning Point USA," Political Research Associates, January 28, 2022, https://politicalresearch.org/2022/01/28/ten-years-turning-point-usa.

Rule Three: Get Real about History

61 *historical record of the rise of White Christian nationalism:* Some of these books include: Anthea Butler's *White Evangelical Racism: The Politics of Morality in America*; Ann Nelson's *Shadow Network: Media, Money, and the Secret Hub of the Radical Right*; Katherine Stewart's *The Power Worshippers: Inside the Dangerous Rise of Religious Nationalism*; Bradley Onishi's *Preparing for War: The Extremist History of White Christian Nationalism—And What Comes Next*; and Kristin Kobes du Mez's *Jesus and John Wayne: How White Evangelicals Corrupted a Faith and Fractured a Nation*.

64 ***Donald Trump is a "wrecking ball to political correctness.":*** Lance Wallnau, *God's Chaos Candidate: Donald J. Trump and the American Unraveling* (Roanoke, TX: Killer Sheep Media, 2016). For an analysis of White evangelical views of Trump as a Cyrus figure, see Adam Gabbatt, "'Unparalleled Privilege': Why White Evangelicals See Trump as Their Savior," *The Guardian*, January 11, 2020, https://www.theguardian.com/us-news/2020/jan/11/donald-trump-evangelical-christians-cyrus-king.

65 *the "Seven Mountain Mandate.":* This is a conservative Christian movement pushing for Christian control over seven "mountains" of family, religion, education, media, entertainment, business, and government. For more on this, see Matthew D. Taylor, *The Violent Take It*

by Force: The Christian Movement That Is Threatening Our Democracy (Minneapolis: Broadleaf Books, 2024).

65 **Butler writes:** Eric C. Miller, "White Evangelical Racism: An Interview with Anthea Butler," *Religion and Politics*, April 20, 2021, https://religionandpolitics.org/2021/04/20/white-evangelical-racism-an-interview-with-anthea-butler/.

70 *The cost of attending a mainline seminary is wildly out of reach:* Tuition at Union Theological Seminary (where I got my MA in biblical studies) is $1,320 per credit for the 2023–2024 academic year: "Tuition and Fees," Union, https://utsnyc.edu/admissions/financial-aid/tuition-fees/.

Meanwhile, graduate tuition at Liberty University ranges from $565–615 per credit (and only $275 for military veterans, and all first-responders get an additional 25 percent discount): Liberty University, *Pursue What Matters*, https://online.flippingbook.com/view/925071094/. Liberty is far from the most affordable option. In 2022, 100 percent of graduates of Faith Baptist Theological Seminary in Ankeny, Ohio, completed their degrees with zero debt: "Faith Baptist Bible College and Theological Seminary Named 'Most Affordable,'" Faith News, Faith Baptist Theological Seminary, June 9, 2022, https://faith.edu/faith-news/faith-baptist-bible-college-and-theological-seminary-named-most-affordable/.

70 *"TOGETHER WE CAN RESTORE AMERICA'S BIBLICAL VALUES.":* All this language is real and straight off the website: "TP USA Faith," TP USA Faith, accessed January 11, 2024, https://tpusafaith.com/.

75 *the following excerpt from Nancy Isenberg's:* Nancy Isenberg, *White Trash: The 400-Year Untold History of Class in America* (New York: Penguin Books, 2017), 34.

77 *the John Brown statue erected by locals:* Thanks, Rev. Dr. Jess Williams, for this lead!: Melissa Greenstein, "Slavery Opponent John Brown's Statue Hit Again by Vandals," *KSHB*, November 20, 2019, https://www.kshb.com/news/local-news/slavery-opponent-john-browns-statue-hit-again-by-vandals.

Rule Four: Know Yourself, Know Your Adversary

86 ***Dr. King said it best:*** Rev. Dr. Martin Luther King Jr. *Where Do We Go from Here: Chaos Or Community?* (Boston: Beacon Press, 1967), 38.

92 ***only 37.7 percent of Americans have a bachelor's degree or higher:*** Tyler Talbott, "The Percentage of Americans with College Degrees in 2023," *College Transitions*, August 12, 2023, https://www.col legetransitions.com/blog/percentage-of-americans-with-college-degrees/#:~:text=In%20the%20Census%20Bureau's%20most, doing%20so%20in%20record%20numbers.

96 ***a robust national network grooming local candidates:*** Steve Rabey, "Two Little-Known Groups Are Training Conservative Legislators and School Board Members," *Baptist News*, August 2, 2023, https:// baptistnews.com/article/two-little-known-groups-are-training-conservative-legislators-and-school-board-members/.

96 ***Faith & Freedom Coalition also lists:*** See Faith & Freedom Coalition website, accessed March 22, 2024, https://www.ffcoalition. com/.

Rule Five: Calculate Your Risks

110 ***In the words of Rev. Dr. Martin Luther King Jr.:*** Martin Luther King Jr., "Nonviolence and Social Change," (The Massey Lectures, Toronto, Ontario, November–December 1967).

Rule Six: Get a Religious Strategy, Even If You Aren't Religious

117 ***popularity of this song surged during the first Gulf War:*** Hat tip to Rev. Dr. Jess Williams, again, for this insight.

125 ***how it looks to read the Bible with the poor:*** Portions of this section I originally preached at St. Timothy's Episcopal Church, Chehalis, WA, October 20, 2019.

127 ***"prohibited from engaging in business or trade":*** Alfred Edersheim, "Travelling in Palestine—Roads, Inns, Hospitality, Custom-House Officers, Taxation, Publicans," chap. 4 in *Sketches of Jewish Social*

Life (Grand Rapids, MI: Christian Classics Ethereal Library, n.d.), https://www.ccel.org/ccel/e/edersheim/sketches/cache/sketches.pdf.

Rule Seven: Rehome Randy

138 ***the vast majority of these are small and getting smaller:*** 2019 data from the Pew Research Center found that Christians are on the decline both in terms of raw numbers as well as share of the US population. Even those who still go to church are going far less often. Millennials who identify as Christians, the youngest generation included in the data, were already down to just 49 percent in 2019. By comparison, the Silent Generation was 84 percent, Boomers were 76 percent, and Gen X was 67 percent. See "In U.S., Decline of Christianity Continues at Rapid Pace," Pew Research Center, October 17, 2019, https://www.pewresearch.org/religion/2019/10/17/in-u-s-decline-of-christianity-continues-at-rapid-pace/.

The churches running counter to this trend are megachurches (those with at least 2,000 members). Though there were an estimated 338,000 churches in America in 2010, their median size was only 75 people on an average Sunday. For more on this, see Warren Bird, PhD, and Scott Thumma, PhD, *Megachurch 2020*, Hartford Institute for Religion Research, 2020, https://faithcommunitiestoday.org/wp-content/uploads/2020/10/Megachurch-Survey-Report_HIRR_FACT-2020.pdf; and Hartford Institute for Religion Research, "Fast Facts about American Religion," http://hirr.hartsem.edu/research/fastfacts/fast_facts.html#:~:text=Hartford%20Institute%20estimates%20there%20are,are%20Catholic%20and%20Orthodox%20churches.

145 ***what the religious landscape might be in your corner of the country:*** For a view of the landscape where you are, check out Niraj Chokshi, "The Religious States of America, in 22 Maps," *Washington Post*, February 26, 2015, https://www.washingtonpost.com/blogs/govbeat/wp/2015/02/26/the-religious-states-of-america-in-22-maps/.

You can also view Christian demographics at the county level, from the 2010 Association of Religion Data Archive study: Alex, "Christianity in the US Counties," Vivid Maps, accessed January 11, 2024, https://vividmaps.com/christianity-us-counties/.

148 *microeconomist Robert Paul Hartley writes:* Robert Paul Hartley and Shailly Gupta Barnes, "Unleashing the Power of Poor and Low-Income Americans: Changing the Political Landscape," Report for the Poor People's Campaign, August 2020, 14, https://www.poorpeoplescampaign.org/wp-content/uploads/2020/08/PPC-Voter-Research-Brief-18.pdf.

149 *Economist Hartley here again:* Hartley and Barnes, 19: "This evidence is also not intended to diminish the impact of voter suppression that might target low-income or minority voters, nor the role of gerrymandering, which has been struck down in some places as unconstitutional. Even though individuals report one reason for not voting, other reasons may also matter, including accessibility."

150 *true of both evangelicals and mainline Christians:* "Statistically, mainliners tend to resemble their (probable) historical namesake, skewing white and relatively wealthy. Their members can also be influential: The lion's share of U.S. presidents—including Barack Obama, who came to Christ in a UCC church, and Donald Trump, who initially identified as Presbyterian—have hailed from mainline traditions at some point in their lives, if not during their presidency." See Jack Jenkins, "What is a Mainline Christian, Anyway?" *Religion News Service*, July 8, 2021, https://religionnews.com/2021/07/08/what-is-a-mainline-christian-anyway/.

150 *have the lowest household incomes:* David Masci, "How Income Varies among U.S. Religious Groups," Pew Research Center, October 11, 2016, https://www.pewresearch.org/short-reads/2016/10/11/how-income-varies-among-u-s-religious-groups/.

151 *Martin Luther's own 1525 advice:* E. G. Rupp and Benjamin Drewery, Martin Luther, Documents of Modern History (London: Edward Arnold, 1970), 121–26, http://individual.utoronto.ca/mmilner/history2p91/primary/rupp6213.htm.

Rule Eight: Stop Blaming People and Start Organizing Them

160 *in the words of two of her friends:* For more of the tribute, see William J. Barber III and Catherine Flowers, "Remembering Pamela Sue Rush: A Death Caused by Structural Poverty," *Facing South*, July 16, 2020, https://www.facingsouth.org/2020/07/remembering-pamela-sue-rush-death-caused-structural-poverty.

Rule Nine: Pledge Allegiance to the Bottom

172 *about the Scottish cattle-rustling border clans:* Wikipedia, s.v. "Border Reivers," last modified January 22, 2024, https://en.wikipedia.org/wiki/Border_reivers.

178 *In a July 2020 interview, Alexandre described her findings:* Amanda Borschel-Dan, "What Do We Know about Nazareth in Jesus' Time? An Archeologist Explains," *The Times of Israel*, July 22, 2020, https://www.timesofisrael.com/listen-what-do-we-know-about-nazareth-in-jesus-time-an-archaeologist-explains/.

179 *the hidden levels of the pits allowed families in Nazareth:* Amanda Borschel-Dan, "LISTEN: What Do We Know about Nazareth in Jesus' Time? An Archaeologist Explains," *Times of Israel*, July 22, 2020, https://www.timesofisrael.com/listen-what-do-we-know-about-nazareth-in-jesus-time-an-archaeologist-explains/.

Rule Ten: Never Forget That the Revolution Comes to Randyland Too

186 *a literal Exodus-to-the-wilderness story:* Richard Grant, "Deep in the Swamps, Archaeologists Are Finding Out How Fugitive Slaves Kept Their Freedom," *Smithsonian Magazine*, September 2016, https://www.smithsonianmag.com/history/deep-swamps-archaeologists-fugitive-slaves-kept-freedom-180960122/.

194 *This system treats injuries to the rich as public crises:* Shailly Gupta Barnes, "Kairos Center Policy Briefing #1: Predictable and

Possible," Kairos Center, May 22, 2020, https://kairoscenter.org/policy-briefing-1-predictable-and-possible/.

194 *US billionaire wealth increased by $485 billion:* "Pandemic Creates New Billionaire Every 30 Hours—Now a Million People Could Fall into Extreme Poverty at the Same Rate in 2022," Oxfam International, May 23, 2022, https://www.oxfam.org/en/press-releases/pandemic-creates-new-billionaire-every-30-hours-now-million-people-could-fall.

195 *Poor People's Campaign released the "Poor People's Moral Budget,":* "Poor People's Moral Budget," Poor People's Campaign, June 15, 2020, https://www.poorpeoplescampaign.org/resource/poor-peoples-moral-budget/.

195 *"the nonviolent army of the poor":* Holly Genovese, "Martin Luther King Jr. and the Black Panther Party Shared Many of the Same Ideologies," *Teen Vogue,* April 4, 2018, https://www.teenvogue.com/story/martin-luther-king-jr-and-the-black-panther-party.